I0121119

"Binna Kandola has pulled off a remarkable feat, delivering such a thorough but also compact study of psychological safety, its uses and significance. He shows how important and subtle cultural issues can be at work. His examples are rich and varied, and the lessons he draws from them are useful and 'actionable.' This highly practical book will equip any manager with modern and humane methods and approaches. This is the guide to psychological safety we have been waiting for."

Stefan Stern, *author and former FT management columnist*

"Suppressing difficult conversations today leads to more difficult conversations and worse situations tomorrow. This excellent and timely book examines these issues through compelling case studies, from the Tour de France to the aviation industry, and provides practical guidance for developing organizational cultures and processes that enable people to speak up."

Dr. Mark Robinson, *Director of the Socio-Technical Centre and Associate Professor, University of Leeds, UK*

"This book offers a thoughtful and well-evidenced guide to building psychologically safe environments at work. Its strength lies in its clarity, its grounding in research, and its practical application to real-world organizational challenges. For those of us who believe inclusion is fundamental to business success, this is an invaluable resource. I highly recommend it."

Nimesh Shah, *CEO Blick Rothenberg*

"This book is a powerful and timely contribution to the field. Grounded in rigorous psychological research—both classic and contemporary—it brings the concept of psychological safety to life in a way that is accessible, practical, and deeply relevant to today's workplaces. From famous studies on group behavior and authority to modern examples from global organizations, it seamlessly connects theory to action. Whether you're a leader, a team member, or a change agent, you'll find insight and inspiration here. I couldn't put it down!"

Chris Yates, *SVP Talent, Equinix*

ACKNOWLEDGMENTS

There are so many people to thank in the writing of this book, and I am deeply appreciative of all the support I've received along the way.

First and foremost, I want to thank my colleagues at Pearn Kandola, whose dedication, expertise, and openness have taught me so much about what it truly means to work in a psychologically safe environment. You have also shown me what I need to do to play my part in fostering that safety, and I am forever grateful for your candor and encouragement. Thank you to Grace Cleere who, in addition to being our senior marketing manager, also provided valuable advice and assistance for *The Godfather* script in Chapter 6.

I also want to express my gratitude for the work of the late Professor Chris Clegg at Leeds University Business School. Chris was a constant source of inspiration, and his passion for understanding and improving organizations continues to influence me to this day.

To the incredibly talented and approachable psychology team at Leeds University Business School—thank you for your support in shaping this book. In particular, I would like to recognize Dr. Matt Davies, Dr. Helen Hughes, and Dr. Mark Robinson, whose insightful conversations during the latter stages of this process helped refine my thinking and improve the final product.

I am also grateful to the British Psychological Society for trusting me to write this book as part of their series. I hope the final product affirms the confidence you placed in me.

A very special thank you to my editor, Hannah Rich, whose constant support and critical feedback made this book possible. Her judgment was something I deeply trusted, and I am incredibly grateful for her availability and guidance throughout this process. Remarkably, all of this support was provided via email—we've never met or spoken directly—but Hannah's presence was felt at every step of the writing process. Marie Hennemann is the very definition of a project manager whose efficiency and clarity of communication made my life a lot easier.

Finally, to my wife, Dr. Jo Kandola, who has been my constant source of advice and security throughout this endeavor. Whenever my energy was flagging, your reassurance and calm perspective lifted me up and kept me moving forward. Thank you for your unwavering belief in me and in this work.

This book reflects decades of collaboration, learning, and support, and it simply wouldn't have been possible without the incredible people mentioned here. To everyone who has contributed to this project—whether through conversations, feedback, inspiration, or encouragement—thank you. Your impact is felt on every page.

WHO AM I AND WHY AM I GIVING THIS ADVICE?

I am a business psychologist and senior partner at Pearn Kandola, a practice based in Oxford with over 40 years of experience working with a wide range of organizations across the private, public, and third sectors. Our clients include some of the most influential organizations in the world, such as Microsoft, NATO, the World Bank, the United Nations, American Express, Oxfam, and British Airways. Over the decades, I have witnessed firsthand how organizations thrive—or falter—depending on the psychological safety they create for their people.

As the founder of a business that has successfully endured and evolved for over four decades, I have learned from both my mistakes and the feedback of my colleagues and clients. Reflecting on both failures and successes has been a cornerstone of my work, enabling me to adapt and improve continually. Without this willingness to analyze and learn, my business would not have stood the test of time.

Throughout my career, I have focused on issues of diversity, equity, and inclusion, starting in the 1980s when the field was known as "equal opportunities." In the 1990s, we also worked in the area of the learning organization, something that did not really take off, but it was an important precursor to the development of psychological safety. In the late 1990s, I began exploring inclusive leadership, analyzing the qualities and skills leaders need to maximize the potential of diverse teams. Over time, our research—based on thousands of participants—revealed that psychological safety was a critical factor for creating truly inclusive environments. This insight led us to integrate psychological safety into our work with organizations, helping leaders and teams foster environments where every voice is valued and people feel safe to contribute.

Beyond my work as a practitioner, I have contributed extensively to the field through twelve books, numerous chapters, and ongoing research. My writings focus on identities in the workplace, prejudice, and the factors that hinder psychological safety. These areas of research are not abstract to me—they are the challenges I have tackled alongside clients, helping them navigate issues of voice, inclusion, and team dynamics.

I have worked with countless leaders and teams, helping them overcome barriers to open communication, resolve conflicts, and improve collaboration. I have seen the transformative power of psychological safety: how it turns struggling teams into high-performing ones and how it enables leaders to unlock the potential of their people. My advice is not theoretical; it is grounded in decades of hands-on experience, research, and learning.

This book is the culmination of everything I have learned about psychological safety—its impact, its challenges, and its power to transform workplaces. My hope is that it provides you with practical insights and tools to create environments where everyone feels safe, valued, and empowered to thrive.

1

WHAT DOES THIS BOOK COVER?

INTRODUCTION

Consider this: over 18,000 academics are members of the Academy of Management, producing a continuous stream of research that circulates within their own circles. These findings reach their peers, but rarely do they make it to the executives who could benefit from them most. During a recent presentation, an academic stood in front of a group of 100 senior executives and asked a simple question: "How many of you are familiar with the concept of psychological safety?" Only two people raised their hands.

Even if we generously assume that the response was off by a factor of ten, we're still left with a glaring issue: psychological safety, though increasingly discussed in certain professional and academic circles, is largely unfamiliar to those at the top of organizations—the very people who need to understand and act on it. This is not a minor gap; it's a striking example of how knowledge essential to organizational health and performance remains out of reach for many leaders.[1]

In recent years, psychological safety has gained some traction thanks to the work of thinkers like Amy Edmondson, whose research has helped bring the concept to the surface. The term is

DOI: 10.4324/9781003501855-1

now widely recognized, and it's often used to capture the essence of what a healthy, open workplace should feel like. But psychological safety has, in some ways, become a cliché—invoked whenever someone feels uncomfortable or unheard, or when their perspective isn't immediately adopted by the group. Without a deeper understanding, grounded in the work of those who first conceptualized it, psychological safety risks becoming a misunderstood buzzword, simplified into a demand for uncritical acceptance rather than a call for genuine openness.

Psychological safety, as originally intended, is not about protecting people from all discomfort; it's about creating an environment where individuals can engage in frank, respectful discussions, where their ideas can be put forward, critiqued, and challenged constructively. True psychological safety requires accepting feedback on one's contributions as much as offering it to others. When practiced fully, it's a dynamic, mutual process of both speaking and listening, giving and receiving, with the aim of building a resilient, innovative, and open workplace.

This book aims to build on the groundwork laid by Edmondson and others, deepening that understanding and making psychological safety an actionable concept for senior leaders. It seeks to close the gap between awareness and real application, providing insights and tools to help executives create workplaces where psychological safety isn't just a term but a lived practice. In doing so, this book will hopefully bridge the divide between knowing about psychological safety and truly understanding what it means to practice it, empowering organizations, leaders, and teams to engage openly and contribute fully.

THE TIMELESS RELEVANCE OF JOHN STUART MILL TO PSYCHOLOGICAL SAFETY

The concept of psychological safety may be a relatively modern one, but the idea of listening to all views and taking action when you see it being done is something that philosophers have been considering for centuries. John Stuart Mill's *On Liberty*,[2] written in 1859, remains a highly influential exploration of individual liberty and its role in societal progress. Its principles resonate strongly with the modern concept of psychological safety—a term that would not be coined for another century. Mill's emphasis on individual freedom, free speech, and his critique of conformity provides a philosophical foundation for understanding and cultivating psychological safety in organizations.

INDIVIDUAL LIBERTY AND ITS CONNECTION TO PSYCHOLOGICAL SAFETY

At the heart of Mill's philosophy is the belief that individuals must be free to pursue their own paths, provided they do not harm others. This aligns directly with the essence of psychological safety, where individuals feel free to speak up, take risks, and express their authentic selves. Mill argued, "The only freedom which deserves the name is that of pursuing our own good in our own way, so long as we do not attempt to deprive others of theirs."[3] He recognized the importance of autonomy and individuality as essential for human and organizational growth.

In workplaces, this translates into environments where employees can challenge ideas, propose innovations, and admit mistakes without fear. When such freedom is absent, creativity and progress are stifled. Mill's insistence on the importance of individual expression is a precursor to the contemporary understanding that diversity of thought and open dialogue drive innovation and adaptability.

THE VALUE OF FREE SPEECH AND DIVERSE OPINIONS

Mill's defense of free speech and open dialogue remains one of the most celebrated aspects of *On Liberty*. He famously stated,

> If all mankind minus one were of one opinion, and only one person were of the contrary opinion, mankind would be no more justified in silencing that one person than he, if he had the power, would be justified in silencing mankind.[4]

This principle highlights the dangers of suppressing dissenting views, as doing so inhibits the testing of ideas and the pursuit of truth.

In the modern workplace, the absence of psychological safety can lead to "groupthink," where consensus-seeking overrides critical thinking. In such environments, innovative ideas are stifled, and organizations become vulnerable to blind spots. Mill's insistence on the value of unpopular or minority opinions mirrors the contemporary understanding that dissenting voices often spark the debates and critical thinking necessary for innovation and problem-solving. Psychological safety ensures these voices are not only tolerated but valued, fostering a culture of intellectual rigor and collective learning.

CONFORMITY AND THE TYRANNY OF THE MAJORITY

One of Mill's central concerns was the "tyranny of the majority," where societal norms suppress individuality and diversity. He warned that social pressures could exert a more insidious form of oppression than governmental control, leading to a stagnant and unthinking society. "Society can and does execute its own mandates," he wrote, "and if it issues wrong mandates instead of right, or any mandates at all in things, with which it, or not to meddle, it practices a social tyranny more formidable than many kinds of political oppression."[5]

In organizational contexts, this tyranny can manifest as conformity, where employees feel compelled to align with dominant perspectives or remain silent to avoid backlash. Such environments hinder psychological safety, discouraging risk-taking and innovation. Mill's critique of conformity underscores the importance of creating spaces where individuals feel safe to challenge norms and propose alternative solutions. By fostering psychological safety, organizations can break free from the constraints of groupthink and leverage the diverse strengths of their teams.

THE HARM PRINCIPLE AND ITS ORGANIZATIONAL IMPLICATIONS

Mill's "harm principle"[6] states that the only justification for restricting individual liberty is to prevent harm to others. This idea has profound implications for psychological safety. In toxic work environments, harm often takes the form of emotional or psychological damage. For instance, punitive feedback, ridicule, or exclusion can silence employees and undermine their confidence. Such behaviors violate Mill's principle by stifling individual expression and harming the collective well-being.

Organizations that prioritize psychological safety actively work to prevent such harm. They foster cultures where feedback is constructive, mistakes are treated as learning opportunities, and respect is paramount. This aligns with Mill's vision of a society that maximizes freedom while minimizing harm, creating conditions for individuals to thrive and contribute meaningfully.

RELEVANCE TO MODERN ORGANIZATIONS

Mill's insights are strikingly relevant in today's complex and fast-changing world. The global economy increasingly values creativity, collaboration, and adaptability—qualities that flourish in psychologically safe environments. Just as Mill argued that liberty and diversity drive societal progress, psychological safety enables organizations to innovate and succeed by leveraging the unique perspectives and talents of their members.

Moreover, Mill's emphasis on individual accountability resonates with the responsibilities of modern leaders. He observed, "A person may cause evil to others not only by his actions but by his inaction and in either case he is justly accountable to them for the injury."[7] This serves as a reminder that fostering psychological safety requires active effort. Leaders must model inclusive behaviors, challenge harmful norms, and create systems that support open communication and trust. It also makes a statement that we all have a part to play in creating psychological safety in our teams and in our organizations

The concepts in this book, therefore, are a development of ideas that thinkers and philosophers have been grappling with for millennia. This represents something deep and profound within us: that we are constantly returning to the idea of our personal freedom and recognizing the dangers of ignoring the minority voices.

STRUCTURE OF THE BOOK

This book is essentially in three parts. Part I, looks at definitions, benefits, and the relationships with other related concepts. It provides answers to the following questions:

- Chapter 2. What is Psychological Safety?
- Chapter 3. Why Should I Pay Attention to It?
- Chapter 4. How Does It Relate to Other Concepts?

The second part of the book looks specifically at the roles of different people in creating psychological safety. It uses some classic social psychology experiments to illustrate how our expressed attitudes are influenced by the people around us. The specific questions these chapters answer are:

- Chapter 5. What Is the Role of the Leader in Fostering Psychological Safety?
- Chapter 6. What If I Am the Only Dissenting Voice in the Team?
- Chapter 7. What Is My Personal Role in Fostering Psychological Safety?
- Chapter 8. Psychological Safety: But for Who?

The third part brings all of the ideas together in order to carry out a systemic, organizational analysis. Checklists are provided so that you have the indicators to be able to carry out organization-wide analyses yourself, or to look at more specific aspects, such as psychological safety in your team, or for a leader to examine strengths and development areas. The specific question being answered is:

- Chapter 9. How Can I Use the Ideas in This Book to Carry Out an Analysis of Psychological Safety in My Organization?

My intention in writing the book is to give you sufficient knowledge to understand what this concept is, but also enough practical guidance for you to be able to use the information to the benefit of your organization, and the people who come to work in it every day.

NOTES

1 William Pasmore (2024). "Foreword 2–Edgar Schein: Learning Through Helping" in Coghlan, D., *Edgar H. Schein: The Artistry of a Reflexive Organizational Scholar-Practitioner.* Taylor & Francis.
2 Mill, J.S. (1859). *On Liberty.* Dover Thrift Editions.
3 P9. Mill, J.S. (1859). *On Liberty.* Dover Thrift Editions.

4 P14 Mill, J.S. (1859). *On Liberty.* Dover Thrift Editions.
5 P4 Mill, J.S. (1859). *On Liberty.* Dover Thrift Editions.
6 P8 Mill, J.S. (1859). *On Liberty.* Dover Thrift Editions.
7 Mill, J.S. (1859). *On Liberty.* Dover Thrift Editions.

PART I
UNDERSTANDING PSYCHOLOGICAL SAFETY

What it is, why it matters, and how it fits into the bigger picture.

This part explains the core concepts, clarifies definitions, and distinguishes psychological safety from related ideas such as trust, engagement, and well-being.

DOI: 10.4324/9781003501855-2

2

WHAT IS PSYCHOLOGICAL SAFETY?

INTRODUCTION

> To whom should I complain? Did I tell this,
> Who would believe me? (Act 2, Scene 4)

These lines from William Shakespeare's *Measure for Measure* capture a moment of despair and helplessness as Isabella, a young novice, faces a terrible choice. Her brother Claudio has been sentenced to death by Angelo, the morally rigid deputy ruler of Vienna, who abuses his authority by offering to spare Claudio only if Isabella agrees to sleep with him. Horrified by the proposition, Isabella realizes that even if she tried to expose Angelo's abuse of power, no one would believe her, given his high status and her vulnerability. Her words express the isolation and fear that arise when someone feels unable to speak out against an injustice. Despite being written over 400 years ago, this dilemma resonates with the concerns raised by the #MeToo movement.

Although the term "psychological safety" had yet to be invented, people experienced the devastating impact of not feeling able to speak up. The vocabulary to describe the experience may have been missing, but the concept was understood through people's emotions and experiences rather than defined language. People

DOI: 10.4324/9781003501855-3

knew that speaking out could lead to punishment, that authority could silence and control, and that societal expectations enforced conformity. Today, we have terms like "psychological safety" and "abuse of power" to help bring these feelings to life. Not possessing the words meant that they couldn't fully explain why these things happened and, consequently, how they might be changed. Now, we can analyze these forces with greater clarity, enabling a path forward to environments where people can express themselves without fear, to the benefit of individuals and organizations.

In this chapter, I will examine key definitions of psychological safety to gain a deeper understanding of its scope and significance. To explore the concept's development and dimensions, I will focus on the contributions of four influential thinkers: Edgar Schein and Warren Bennis in the 1960s, William Kahn in the 1990s, and Amy Edmondson from the late 1990s onward. Their work represents three pivotal stages in the evolution of psychological safety, each building on prior insights while introducing unique perspectives that expand our comprehension of the concept. These thinkers not only influenced their own eras but have also shaped modern interpretations and applications of psychological safety in today's workplaces.

While more recent trends often frame psychological safety primarily as a team-level issue affecting individuals, I aim to demonstrate that it also has a critical organizational dimension. Providing a broader organizational context enables us to explore the deeper, systemic factors that foster or undermine psychological safety.

DEFINING PSYCHOLOGICAL SAFETY

There have been many ways of defining psychological safety, and a few of the more recent definitions are provided in Table 2.1.

Table 2.1 *Sample of Definitions of Psychological Safety*

Definition	Reference
"Psychological safety is a climate which encourages provisional tries and which tolerates failure without retaliation, renunciation, or guilt."[1]	Schein, E.H., & Bennis, W.G. (1965). *Personal and Organizational Change Through Group Methods: The Laboratory Approach.* Wiley.
"Sense of being able to show and employ self without fear of negative consequences to self-image, status, or career."[2]	Kahn, W.A. (1990). Psychological conditions of personal engagement and disengagement at work. *Academy of Management Journal, 33*(4), pp. 692–724.
"A shared belief held by members of a team that the team is safe for interpersonal risk taking."[3]	Edmondson, A. (1999). Psychological safety and learning behavior in work teams. *Administrative Science Quarterly, 44*(2), pp. 350–383.
"In a psychologically safe work environment, employees feel that their colleagues will not reject people for being themselves or saying what they think, respect each other's competence, are interested in each other as people, have positive intentions to one another, are able to engage in constructive conflict or confrontation, and feel that it is safe to experiment and take risks."[4]	Newman, A., Donohue, R., & Eva, N. (2017). Psychological safety: A systematic review of the literature. *Human Resource Management Review, 27*(3), pp. 521–535.
"Psychological safety as a cognitive state necessary for learning and change to take place."[5]	Frazier, M.L., Fainshmidt, S., Klinger, R.L., Pezeshkan, A., & Vracheva, V. (2017). Psychological safety: A meta-analytic review and extension. *Personnel Psychology, 70*(1), pp. 113–165.

(Continued)

Table 2.1 (Continued)

Definition	Reference
"Psychological safety is defined as a person's observations of the outcome of taking interpersonal risks at the workplace."[6]	Opoku, M.A., Choi, S.B., & Kang, S.W. (2020). Psychological safety in Ghana: empirical analyses of antecedents and consequences. *International Journal of Environmental Research and Public Health*, *17*(1), p. 214.
"In a broad sense, psychological safety is considered an aspect of the organisational environment. It was also recognised, however, that it may be beneficial to measure psychological safety at an individual level as players may have differing perceptions of psychological safety in their environment."[7]	Vella, S.A., Mayland, E., Schweickle, M.J., Sutcliffe, J.T., McEwan, D., & Swann, C. (2024). Psychological safety in sport: A systematic review and concept analysis. *International Review of Sport and Exercise Psychology*, *17*(1), pp. 516–539.
"In a psychologically safe environment, individuals feel free to take risks without fear of retribution."[8]	Bean, C., Harlow, M., Mosher, A., Fraser-Thomas, J., & Forneris, T (2018). Assessing differences in athlete-reported outcomes between high and low-quality youth sport programs. *Journal of Applied Sport Psychology*, *30*(4), pp. 456–472.
"A belief that the team is safe for interpersonal risk-taking, such as asking for help, admitting one's errors, or seeking feedback from others."[9]	Fransen, K., McEwan, D., & Sarkar, M. (2020). The impact of identity leadership on team functioning and well-being in team sport: Is psychological safety the missing link? *Psychology of Sport and Exercise*, *51*, p. 101763.
"Psychological safety is characterised by the absence of threat or harm."[10]	Vakira, E., Shereni, N.C., Ncube, C.M., & Ndlovu, N. (2023). The effect of inclusive leadership on employee engagement, mediated by psychological safety in the hospitality industry. *Journal of Hospitality and Tourism Insights*, *6*(2).

(*Continued*)

Table 2.1 (Continued)

Definition	Reference
"How people perceive potential threats or rewards when they take interpersonal risks at work. In a psychologically safe work environment, people tend to be less defensive and focus on accomplishing team goals and preventing problems, instead of just protecting themselves. They feel at ease offering original ideas, sharing different viewpoints, asking questions or admitting mistakes, knowing that they won't face punishment or ridicule from their colleagues."[11]	Wietrak, E., & Gifford, J. (2024). *Trust and Psychological Safety: An Evidence Review.* Chartered Institute of Personnel and Development.

From these statements it is possible to identify the themes that connect them:

- **Freedom from Fear of Negative Consequences**: Across definitions, psychological safety implies a lack of fear regarding personal or professional repercussions, such as damage to self-image, status, or career.
- **Comfort in Taking Risks**: Because of the first theme, people feeling secure enough to take interpersonal risks, such as sharing ideas, admitting mistakes, and providing feedback, without fear of ridicule or retribution.
- **Supportive Relationships and Environment**: Trust, respect, and supportive interpersonal relationships are essential components that enable psychological safety at all levels.
- **Learning and Growth**: Psychologically safe environments foster learning, change, and constructive conflict, all of which enable individuals and teams to grow and innovate.

Table 2.2 *Definitions of Psychological Safety at Different Levels*

Focus	Definition	Indicators
Individual	Psychological safety at the individual level is experienced as the personal freedom to express oneself authentically without fear of negative consequences to self-image, status, or career.	Individuals feel comfortable being themselves, admitting mistakes, and sharing their thoughts.
Team	Psychological safety at the team level is a shared belief that the team environment fosters mutual respect, trust, and openness, where members feel valued and comfortable sharing ideas, concerns, and feedback.	It is characterized by inclusive communication, constructive collaboration, appreciation of contributions, and a commitment to learning and collective success.
Organizational	At the organizational level, psychological safety is a climate or culture that tolerates failure without retaliation and encourages risk-taking, learning, and innovation.	This level relies on supportive leadership and inclusive policies that prioritize communication, engagement, and the absence of threat or harm.

- But we can also see that these definitions approach psychological safety from the angle of the individual, the team, and the organization. I have used these definitions to create ones for each of these three levels (Table 2.2).

INDIVIDUAL LEVEL

At the individual level, psychological safety is characterized by a person's sense of security in being their authentic self without fear of negative consequences to their self-image, career, or status. It is about having the personal confidence to engage openly, express thoughts, ask questions, and admit mistakes without fear of ridicule or retribution. This highlights the internal experience of psychological safety. For all of us, psychological safety at the level of the individual is deeply personal, allowing us to focus on our tasks and relationships without defensive behaviors.

This individual perspective sets the groundwork for safety at other levels, as each person's experience influences their interactions within teams.

TEAM LEVEL

Psychological safety at the team level is a shared belief that the team environment fosters mutual respect, trust, and openness, where members feel valued and comfortable sharing ideas, concerns, and feedback. In other words, it is not just about individual confidence but about team-working. It's a shared perception that the group is supportive, open, and respectful. No one will be punished or humiliated for voicing ideas, concerns, or mistakes. This team-level view is crucial for enabling collaboration and innovation, as it creates an environment where team members feel free to challenge ideas, ask for help, and experiment without fear of negative repercussions. A psychologically safe team can engage in constructive conflict and leverage diverse viewpoints to enhance problem-solving and creativity.

ORGANIZATIONAL LEVEL

At the organizational level, psychological safety refers to the overall climate or culture that fosters open communication, learning, and risk-taking. It is cultivated through leadership practices and organizational policies that encourage risk-taking and learning, balanced with respectful communication and inclusivity across all levels. Maintaining this balance can be delicate, and leaders play a critical role in setting expectations and modeling behaviors. An organizational focus on psychological safety is essential for sustaining it over time and across teams. In doing so, it creates a consistent environment that reinforces safety as a fundamental principle, embedded in the organization's values, practices, and support structures.

Psychological safety is not a monolithic concept but rather one that develops at the individual, team, and organizational levels while remaining interconnected.

To foster psychological safety effectively, it is crucial to examine and address it across each of the three levels: organizational, team, and individual. By doing this, organizations can establish a culture where employees feel valued, included, and engaged, capable of contributing their best ideas and efforts within a supportive and secure environment.

This approach helps bridge gaps in the current literature that often focuses predominantly on the team or individual level, overlooking the organizational culture in which they work.

This multi-level framework should enable an analysis of how psychological safety operates across these levels and interacts to influence outcomes like employee engagement, inclusion, productivity, innovation, and ethical conduct. As we will see, this perspective can guide practical applications, helping organizations recognize that fostering psychological safety is neither a one-size-fits-all effort nor one where they can merely copy what others have done. Instead, it requires attention to each level's unique needs.

DEVELOPMENT OF THE CONCEPT

I want to examine briefly the contributions made by some key thought leaders who, between them, have helped us to understand the concept of psychological safety and have explored its breadth and depth. Edgar Schein and Warren Bennis laid the groundwork, introducing the idea that a psychologically safe environment encourages openness, learning, and resilience across the organization. William A. Kahn, in contrast, was focused more on the individual, exploring how each person's subjective experience of psychological safety impacts their engagement and performance. This was an important shift going from the macro to the micro level because it showed how psychological safety is personally felt and experienced, highlighting the importance of creating conditions that allow each individual to bring their full self to work. Finally, Amy Edmondson's transformative work on team-level safety bridges these two perspectives by showing how team norms and group interactions create the immediate social context in which psychological safety is either fostered or undermined.

I am drawn to these thinkers not only because of their influence but because each provides a distinct and interconnected piece to the puzzle. By examining psychological safety through the lenses of organization, team, and individual, they enable us to appreciate how these layers interact to create truly safe environments.

KEY CONTRIBUTORS 1: EDGAR SCHEIN AND WARREN BENNIS

Psychological safety, a term now central to discussions of organizational behavior, was first conceptualized by Edgar Schein and Warren Bennis in 1965. In their work, *Personal and Organizational Change Through Group Methods*,[12] they examined how creating a safe environment in organizational settings could facilitate change, adaptability, and innovation. Given their undoubted prominence in the literature, it came as a bit of a surprise to see that in a book of nearly 400 pages, less than one of them is devoted to psychological safety specifically.

Their focus is on change in organizations, what promotes it and what inhibits it. Effective group functioning rests on the presence of an environment where each member feels able to participate openly. Change will not happen when team members become guarded, withholding insights or concerns due to a fear of being judged. This fear, in turn, breeds a culture of silence, stifling creativity and problem-solving. They argued that only in an atmosphere free from interpersonal risks can organizations harness the full potential of collective intelligence, thereby fostering innovation and adaptability. Psychological safety was particularly helpful in achieving one part of their change, namely that of "unfreezing." "In order for unfreezing to lead to an increased desire to learn, rather than to a heightened anxiety, where the individual is immobilised or impervious to new inputs, an environment must be created with maximum psychological safety."[13] The concept was important to their work but not central to it. Nevertheless, the descriptions of the conditions that need to exist for change to be implemented effectively can be easily applied to those required for psychological safety. Their work also meant we had a form of words to express something that was understood emotionally but could not really be articulated beyond that. Now there was something that could be described and analyzed more rigorously.

They also observed that organizational change often feels inherently destabilizing for individuals. People resist change not solely because of the change itself, but due to the perceived risks associated with departing from established routines. Psychological safety, in this context, becomes essential for engaging employees in the change process. When individuals feel secure, they are more willing to embrace experimentation, challenge the status quo, and adapt to new processes. Without this, change initiatives are likely to encounter resistance, driven by an underlying fear of personal consequences. Leaders have their part to play in this by involving and empowering their teams.

Central to their work was the concept of learning organizations, where continuous learning and adaptation are embedded in the culture. Learning organizations foster environments in which individuals are encouraged to question assumptions and explore novel solutions. This mindset allows organizations to remain agile and resilient, especially in times of uncertainty. Power and entrenched cultural norms often stand in the way, with hierarchical structures particularly prone to fostering environments of compliance rather than openness.

The learning organization was popularized by Peter Senge in his book *The Fifth Discipline*.[14] Here he took a systems thinking, holistic approach to his analysis of organizations encompassing the systems and processes as well as role of leaders, teams, and the individual. My former business partner Michael Pearn co-wrote *Tools for a Learning Organisation* with Chris Mulrooney. Their descriptors of a learning organization include:

- Opportunities to experiment without suffering serious consequences.
- Incidental learning, or learning from everyday experience and debate.
- People being encouraged to question the way things are done.
- Mistakes being treated as learning opportunities.
- Leaders who are generally receptive to new ideas.

We can see the overlap with psychological safety.

Schein and Bennis laid the groundwork for contemporary thought on organizational learning and subsequently psychological safety. They emphasized that reducing interpersonal risks is not a soft, discretionary aspect of management but a critical enabler of organizational resilience and innovation.

KEY CONTRIBUTORS 2: WILLIAM A. KAHN

William Kahn's exploration of psychological safety, though more focused on the individual experience, adds considerable depth to our understanding of this concept. Kahn's work centered on personal engagement—the idea that individuals feel fully present in their roles when they can express their true selves without fear. He argues that psychological safety is a prerequisite for this kind of engagement, as it allows individuals to, in the modern day phrase, bring their whole selves to work, integrating their physical, cognitive, and emotional selves in a way that makes their contributions meaningful. His work is seen as influential in the field of psychological safety, but we should also acknowledge that his ideas have filtered into our understanding of inclusion in today's workplaces.

For Kahn, personal engagement is not static; individuals adjust their level of engagement based on the extent of safety they feel in a given moment. When people sense that they can express themselves without negative repercussions, they are likely to engage deeply with their tasks. Conversely, in the absence of safety, they disengage, protecting themselves by withholding their true selves.

Kahn provided examples from his studies, such as a scuba-diving instructor who fully engages with his students by sharing his passion for the ocean, embodying a true connection between his identity and role. This full engagement, according to Kahn, is only possible when individuals feel psychologically safe.

Kahn identified three psychological conditions essential to engagement: meaningfulness, safety, and availability. Among these, psychological safety stands out as the bedrock, enabling individuals to participate authentically. This safety is influenced by multiple factors within the work environment, including interpersonal relationships, group dynamics, management style, and organizational norms. Supportive relationships create a sense of security, allowing people to experiment and take risks. By contrast, strained relationships lead to withdrawal, as individuals become cautious and defensive.

Informal roles and authority shape individuals' sense of safety. He observed that in hierarchical structures, employees closer to authority figures feel more secure and engaged, while those in marginalized positions experience vulnerability. Similarly, management style plays a critical role; supportive, consistent management fosters an environment where individuals feel encouraged to take initiative, while overbearing management leads to disengagement. Kahn also noted that organizational norms provide predictability and contribute to psychological safety, though they can limit individual expression if overly restrictive.

He is often described as taking the individual's perspective, but in truth, it is a multi-level approach to psychological safety, showing that personal engagement is deeply influenced by the broader work environment. I am drawn to his work because he bridged psychological safety with the modern concept of inclusivity, arguing that people need a supportive, trusting environment to bring their full selves to work.

KEY CONTRIBUTORS 3: AMY EDMONDSON

To understand the essence of psychological safety, it's essential to look at the work of its biggest pioneer, Amy Edmondson. A professor at Harvard Business School and an acclaimed thought leader in organizational behavior, Edmondson's work has fundamentally changed how we think about teamwork, learning, and innovation in the modern workplace. Her curiosity about why some teams excel while others falter led her to uncover a simple yet profound truth: that the key to success lies not just in *what* teams do but in *how* they interact.

Edmondson's professional journey is as fascinating as her research. She began her career as a chief engineer for renowned architect and inventor Buckminster Fuller, where she first observed the dynamics of teams tackling highly creative, interdisciplinary challenges. This sparked her lifelong fascination with how people work together to solve problems.

Amy Edmondson's work on psychological safety has profoundly shaped how organizations approach collaboration, learning, and innovation. Her focus on the team as the central unit of organizational effectiveness is both practical and timely, reflecting the realities of modern work where adaptability, open communication, and collective problem-solving are essential. Across her extensive research and writing, Edmondson has explored the mechanisms that make teams succeed, particularly in her books: *The Fearless*

Organization and *Teaming.* These two works provide complementary perspectives on how psychological safety fosters high performance, innovation, and resilience in teams. Her work has brought psychological safety into mainstream business discourse, where it is increasingly recognized as an essential ingredient for team performance, learning, and innovation.

Central to Edmondson's framework is the concept of voice. She argues that psychological safety creates an environment where individuals feel empowered to speak up, a crucial element for catching errors early and fostering innovation. In fear-based cultures, individuals remain silent, calculating that the cost of speaking up is too high. Edmondson emphasizes that psychological safety helps individuals perceive their voice as not just tolerated but essential for team success.

Edmondson also explores learning from mistakes as a key outcome of psychological safety. In high-stakes environments, like healthcare, reporting errors without fear can prevent harm and improve patient care. Her studies revealed that teams with high psychological safety report more errors—not because they make more mistakes, but because they feel safe to disclose them. This approach encourages a culture of learning, turning failures into opportunities for growth.

Leadership, in Edmondson's view, is the linchpin of psychological safety. She proposes that leaders must set the stage by framing tasks in ways that clarify their complexity and interdependence. Leaders must also invite participation, demonstrating humility by signaling that they don't have all the answers. Edmondson introduces the concept of "blameless reporting," which encourages reporting without fear of reprisal, fostering a culture of continuous learning.

Finally, Edmondson connects psychological safety to innovation and performance. She argues that safety is essential for productive conflict—open, constructive disagreements that lead to better outcomes. Teams with psychological safety can harness diverse viewpoints, preventing groupthink and enabling comprehensive decision-making. For Edmondson, psychological safety is not a luxury or a soft element of management; it is fundamental to organizational health in a complex, competitive environment.

TEN THINGS THAT PSYCHOLOGICAL SAFETY IS NOT

In her book *iGen*, Professor Jean Twenge at San Diego University writes about intergenerational differences, and the title refers to the Internet Generation. One of the things that Twenge remarks upon is how

> Wanting to feel safe all of the time can also lead to wanting to protect against emotional upset—the concern with "emotional safety" … That can include preventing bad experiences, side-stepping situations that might be uncomfortable, and avoiding people with ideas different from your own.[15]

This approach has also been labeled as "safetyism."[16]

If people don't understand psychological safety beyond the term itself, there is a real danger that it becomes misinterpreted in the workplace. So it is worthwhile, just in case psychological safety becomes a reason for avoiding uncomfortable conversations, to explain what psychological safety is not.

1. **Psychological Safety Is Not About Being Nice**: Psychological safety is often misinterpreted as creating an environment where everyone is always nice. While a polite workplace is important, psychological safety means fostering open dialogue and candor, which sometimes requires uncomfortable but necessary conversations. Simply being "nice" can stifle honest feedback and prevent genuine problem-solving.[17]
2. **Psychological Safety Is Not a Guarantee of Comfort**: Many assume psychological safety means always feeling

comfortable, but true psychological safety allows team members to voice concerns and take risks, even when it's uncomfortable. Edmondson states that discomfort is inherent in learning, and psychological safety doesn't eliminate it; instead, it ensures people aren't punished for taking risks.[18]

3. **Psychological Safety Is Not About Lowering Standards**: Psychological safety is sometimes confused with an acceptance of the way a team does its work. For example, where people are so comfortable with one another that they become too casual in their duties. Psychological safety does not excuse low performance and instead ensures that people feel safe enough to acknowledge mistakes and learn from them.[19]

4. **Psychological Safety Is Not the Absence of Accountability**: Psychological safety does not mean a lack of accountability; rather, it complements it. Employees can expect to be held responsible for their work, but they feel secure enough to admit errors without fear of retribution, which fosters improvement and growth.[20]

5. **Psychological Safety Is Not a Shield Against Criticism**: Psychological safety encourages constructive feedback rather than shielding individuals from it. A psychologically safe environment allows for honest and constructive criticism aimed at development rather than protection from all forms of critique.[21]

6. **Psychological Safety Is Not About People Agreeing**: It is a misinterpretation to think that disagreement creates unsafe environments. Having our views challenged and being able to challenge other ideas means that we can arrive at solutions that are more effective. Robust conversations, conducted respectfully, enable learning and growth to take place. It's about empowering people to voice differing opinions, which promotes innovation and prevents groupthink.[22]

7. **Psychological Safety Is Not a Lack of Hierarchy**: Psychological safety does not imply that hierarchies are

eliminated in an organization. Leaders play a crucial role in creating safe environments by modeling openness and fallibility. Hierarchies can exist in psychologically safe workplaces as long as leaders encourage open communication across levels.[23]

8. **Psychological Safety Is Not Permission to Slacken Off**: Psychological safety is sometimes mistaken as permission to reduce effort or commitment. Kahn clarifies that in psychologically safe environments, individuals are more likely to be fully engaged because they know they can try and fail without fear of punishment. It supports taking initiative and learning through effort rather than allowing reduced engagement.[24]

9. **Psychological Safety Is Not Endless Debate or Unproductive Talk**: Some managers worry that psychological safety will lead to excessive, unproductive conversations that slow progress. However, Amy Edmondson and Tijs Besieux explain that psychological safety does not encourage endless chatter; it allows productive contributions that add value while still aiming for efficiency and balance.[25]

10. **Psychological Safety Is Not About Avoiding Difficult Workplace Conversations**: Psychological safety involves addressing all workplace matters openly, including sensitive topics like race or ethics. Psychologically safe environments allow discussions across various subjects and enable openness in all aspects of work, including social and identity issues that impact colleagues.[26]

In summary, psychological safety is often misunderstood as being synonymous with "niceness" or comfort, but these are false associations. True psychological safety involves candid conversations, openness to risk, and a willingness to embrace discomfort for the sake of growth and innovation.

Leaders and organizations must move beyond superficial politeness and efficiency concerns to foster environments where constructive dialogue and vulnerability are not only accepted but encouraged. By balancing candor with respect and teaching employees how to communicate productively, organizations can create spaces where psychological safety flourishes—leading to improved learning, performance, and collaboration.

KEY POINTS

Psychological safety is not a new concept, but its importance in modern workplaces has become increasingly recognized. This chapter explored how the term has evolved over time, from its early roots in Schein and Bennis's work on organizational change to William Kahn's focus on individual engagement and Amy Edmondson's groundbreaking research on team dynamics. At its core, psychological safety is about creating environments where individuals feel secure to express themselves, share ideas, and acknowledge mistakes without fear of humiliation or retaliation. It exists at the intersection of individual experiences, team interactions, and organizational culture, making it a multi-level construct essential for fostering trust, openness, and collaboration across the workplace. Each of these levels is interconnected, demonstrating that individual confidence builds the foundation for team success, which in turn thrives within an enabling organizational culture.

A key stepping stone in understanding psychological safety is the concept of the learning organization, popularized by Peter Senge. Schein and Bennis introduced the idea that psychologically safe environments are critical for enabling change and adaptability within organizations. They recognized that fear stifles creativity and innovation, while psychological safety unlocks the potential for experimentation, open dialogue, and collective problem-solving. The learning organization embodies many of these principles, encouraging individuals to question assumptions, treat mistakes as opportunities for growth, and engage in continuous learning. This approach aligned closely with the attributes of psychologically safe workplaces, but, after a brief period of popularity, it waned perhaps because it may have been too complex to integrate into organizations.

While this chapter focused on defining and contextualizing psychological safety, the next chapter delves into its transformative benefits.

GLOSSARY

Psychological safety is about creating environments where individuals feel secure to express themselves, share ideas, and acknowledge mistakes without fear of humiliation or retaliation. It exists at the intersection of individual experiences, team interactions, and organizational culture, making it a multi-level construct essential for fostering trust, openness, and collaboration across the workplace.

- Psychological safety at the **individual level** is characterized by a person's sense of security in being their authentic self without fear of negative consequences to their self-image, career, or status.
- Psychological safety at the **team level** is a shared belief that the team environment fosters mutual respect, trust, and openness, where members feel valued and comfortable sharing ideas, concerns, and feedback.
- Psychological safety at the **organizational level** refers to the overall climate or culture that fosters open communication, learning, and risk-taking. It is cultivated through leadership practices and organizational policies that encourage risk-taking and learning, balanced with respectful communication and inclusivity across all levels.

NOTES

1 Schein, E.H., & Bennis, W.G. (1965). *Personal and Organizational Change Through Group Methods: The Laboratory Approach.* New York: Wiley.

2 Kahn, W.A. (1990). Psychological conditions of personal engagement and disengagement at work. *Academy of Management Journal, 33*(4), pp. 692–724.

3 Edmondson, A. (1999). Psychological Safety and Learning Behavior in Work Teams. *Administrative Science Quarterly, 44*(2), pp. 350–383.

4 Newman, A., Donohue, R., & Eva, N. (2017). Psychological safety: A systematic review of the literature. *Human Resource Management Review, 27*(3), pp. 521–535.

5 Frazier, M.L., Fainshmidt, S., Klinger, R.L., Pezeshkan, A., & Vracheva, V. (2017). Psychological safety: A meta-analytic review and extension. *Personnel Psychology, 70*(1), pp. 113–165.

6 Opoku, M.A., Choi, S.B., & Kang, S.W. (2020). Psychological safety in Ghana: empirical analyses of antecedents and consequences. *International Journal of Environmental Research and* Public Health, 17(1), p. 214.

7 Vella, S.A., Mayland, E., Schweickle, M.J., Sutcliffe, J.T., McEwan, D., & Swann, C. (2024). Psychological safety in sport: A systematic review and concept analysis. *International Review of Sport and Exercise Psychology, 17*(1), pp. 516–539.

8 Bean, C., Harlow, M., Mosher, A., Fraser-Thomas, J., & Forneris, T. (2018). Assessing differences in athlete-reported outcomes between high- and low-quality youth sport programs. *Journal of Applied Sport Psychology, 30*(4), pp. 456–472.

9 Fransen, K., McEwan, D., & Sarkar, M. (2020). The impact of identity leadership on team functioning and well-being in team sport: Is psychological safety the missing link? *Psychology of Sport and Exercise, 51,* p. 101763.

10 Vakira, E., Shereni, N.C., Ncube, C.M., & Ndlovu, N. (2023). The effect of inclusive leadership on employee engagement, mediated by psychological safety in the hospitality industry. *Journal of Hospitality and Tourism Insights, 6*(2).

11 Wietrak, E., & Gifford, J. (2024). *Trust and Psychological Safety: An Evidence Review.* Chartered Institute of Personnel and Development.

12 Schein, E.H., & Bennis, W.G. (1965). *Personal and Organizational Change through Group Methods: The Laboratory Approach.* Wiley.

13 Schein, E.H., & Bennis, W.G. (1965). *Personal and Organizational Change through Group Methods: The Laboratory Approach.* Wiley, p. 44.

14 Senge, P.M. (1990) *The Fifth Discipline: The Art and Practice of The Learning Organization*. Random House.

15 Twenge, Jean M. (2017). *IGen: Why Today's Super-Connected Kids Are Growing Up Less Rebellious, More Tolerant, Less Happy—and Completely Unprepared for Adulthood (and What This Means for the Rest of Us)*. First Atria Books hardcover edition. Atria Books, p. 153.

16 Lukianoff, Greg, & Haidt, Jonathan (2018). *The Coddling of the American Mind: How Good Intentions and Bad Ideas Are Setting up a Generation for Failure*. Allen Lane, p. 29.

17 Edmondson, A.C. (2002). *Managing the Risk of Learning: Psychological Safety in Work Teams*. Division of Research, Harvard Business School, pp. 255–275.

18 Edmondson, A.C. (2018). *The Fearless Organization: Creating Psychological Safety in the Workplace for Learning, Innovation, and Growth*. Wiley.

19 Edmondson, A.C., Kramer, R.M., & Cook, K.S. (2004). Psychological safety, trust, and learning in organizations: A group-level lens. Trust and distrust in organizations. *Dilemmas and Approaches*, *12*(2004), pp. 239–272.

20 Edmondson, A.C. (2018). *The Fearless Organization: Creating Psychological Safety in the Workplace for Learning, Innovation, and Growth*. Wiley.

21 Gallo, A. (2023). What is psychological safety? *Harvard Business Review*, 15.

22 Lukianoff, Greg, & Haidt, Jonathan. *The Coddling of the American Mind: How Good Intentions and Bad Ideas Are Setting up a Generation for Failure*. Allen Lane, 2018, p. 29.

23 Binyamin, G., Friedman, A., & Carmeli, A. (2018). Reciprocal care in hierarchical exchange: Implications for psychological safety and innovative behaviors at work. *Psychology of Aesthetics, Creativity, and the Arts*, *12*(1), p. 79.

24 Kahn, W.A. (1990). Psychological conditions of personal engagement and disengagement at work. *Academy of Management Journal*, *33*(4), 692–724.

25 Hosseini, E. and Sabokro, M. (2022). A systematic literature review of the organizational voice. *Interdisciplinary Journal of Management Studies*

(formerly known as *Iranian Journal of Management Studies*), *15*(2), pp. 227–252.

26 Williams, J.D., Woodson, A.N., and Wallace, T.L. (2016). "Can we say the n-word?": Exploring psychological safety during race talk. *Research in Human Development*, *13*(1), pp. 15–31.

FURTHER READING

Brown, B., 2018. *Dare to lead: Brave work. Tough conversations. Whole hearts.* Random House.

Edmondson, Amy C., 2019. *The fearless organization: Creating psychological safety in the workplace for learning, innovation, and growth.* Wiley.

Edmondson, Amy C. and Harvey, Jean-François, 2023. *Right kind of wrong: The science of failing well.* Atria Books.

Lukianoff, G. and Haidt, J., 2018. *The coddling of the American mind: How good intentions and bad ideas are setting up a generation for failure.* Allen Lane.

Video: Amy Edmondson—Building a Psychologically Safe Workplace (TEDx Talks). https://www.youtube.com/watch?v=LhoLuui9gX8

3

WHY SHOULD I PAY ATTENTION TO PSYCHOLOGICAL SAFETY AT WORK?

INTRODUCTION

Imagine a workplace where every voice is heard, where team members don't fear ridicule when suggesting a bold idea, and where mistakes are seen not as failures but as steps toward growth. This chapter is an invitation—and a challenge—to reimagine what's possible in your organization by embracing psychological safety. For those who believe in strict hierarchies and traditional power dynamics, this might seem counterintuitive. But consider this: the most innovative, resilient organizations today are the ones breaking away from those old norms. They're creating spaces where people feel free to speak up, experiment, and learn together.

In today's rapidly evolving work environment, where innovation, adaptability, and employee engagement are essential for success, psychological safety has emerged as a fundamental requirement for high-performing teams and organizations. Let this chapter serve as a guide through the practical and impactful changes that psychological safety can bring. I'll share with you how fostering such an environment can enhance individual well-being, strengthen team collaboration, and ultimately support organizational growth. By

DOI: 10.4324/9781003501855-4

the end, I hope to have provided not only a compelling case for why psychological safety matters but also a clear sense of how to begin integrating it meaningfully into your workplace. This is an invitation to look closely at how we work together and to consider small, thoughtful adjustments that could make a profound difference.

In this chapter, I will explore the multi-layered benefits of psychological safety, diving into how it shapes the experiences of individuals, teams, and entire organizations. We'll begin by examining what psychological safety brings to each level, from the personal confidence and engagement of individuals to the collaborative power of teams and, finally, to the overall resilience and adaptability of the organization.

But understanding the benefits is only part of the picture. We'll also look at the foundational elements—what we might call the "preconditions" or "antecedents"—that need to be in place for psychological safety to take root and genuinely thrive within an organization. These are the crucial conditions that help foster an environment where people feel comfortable sharing ideas, taking risks, and supporting one another.

Finally, I will outline some initial steps that can guide any organization toward cultivating a healthier, more productive working environment. This exploration isn't one of quick fixes; it's a commitment to growth and continuous improvement. By the end, I hope you'll be encouraged, if not inspired not only to see the potential of psychological safety but also to start nurturing it in your own workplace—taking meaningful steps toward a culture where everyone can bring their best, every day.

BENEFITS OF PSYCHOLOGICAL SAFETY FOR INDIVIDUALS

There are many benefits for individuals working in psychologically safe environments, including enhancing mental health and well-being, fostering engagement and commitment, and supporting growth and learning.

ENHANCING MENTAL HEALTH AND WELL-BEING

Psychological safety plays a significant role in improving individual mental health by reducing anxiety, fostering resilience, and encouraging help-seeking behavior. In work settings where individuals feel psychologically safe, they experience lower stress levels and are more likely to express concerns, seek assistance, and openly discuss vulnerabilities.

- **Reduced Anxiety and Stress**: One of the primary benefits of psychological safety is the reduction in anxiety and stress. When individuals know they can speak up without fear of retaliation or judgment, they feel less stressed. For example, in a sports setting, psychological safety allowed athletes to operate without fear of being reprimanded for mistakes, thus lowering their stress and anxiety levels.[1] Similarly, employees in psychologically safe workplaces feel more at ease to raise concerns or ask questions, contributing to a healthier mental state.
- **Encouraging Help-Seeking Behavior**: Psychological safety removes the stigma associated with seeking help and disclosing mental health challenges. A study on athletes found that individuals in psychologically safe environments are more likely to disclose vulnerabilities and seek support for mental health issues.[2] This open culture reduces the stigma around mental health, felt especially by elite athletes, and allows individuals to access resources and assistance when they need it.

  For example, in high-stakes environments such as healthcare, psychological safety allows staff to communicate openly about potential issues without fear of blame. Staff in psychologically safe teams reported more potential medication errors, which showed an overriding concern for preventing harm to patients and alleviating personal anxiety. This openness also encourages staff to seek clarification and assistance whenever uncertain, knowing that their team supports a culture of learning over punishment.[3]

- **Resilience and Coping**: Psychological safety also bolsters individual resilience. By fostering an environment where individuals can express their struggles and receive support, psychological safety helps build a robust support network that individuals can rely on during difficult times. Athletes who felt safe expressing challenges to coaches and teammates exhibited greater resilience, as they felt they had a supportive community behind them.[4] This is equally relevant in corporate environments, where employees who feel supported are more likely to persevere through challenges and recover from setbacks more quickly. An examination of sales teams during COVID-19 lockdowns found that creating an environment of psychological safety enabled the team members to cope well with the uncertainty and disruption that they were confronted with.[5]

FOSTERING ENGAGEMENT AND COMMITMENT

Engagement and commitment are significantly enhanced in environments where psychological safety is high. When employees feel they can be themselves and share their ideas freely, they are more likely to be engaged in their work, satisfied with their roles, and committed to their organization.

- **Work Engagement**: Psychological safety allows individuals to be fully engaged in their roles. According to William Kahn, when individuals feel safe, they are more likely to engage themselves emotionally, cognitively, and physically in their work.[6] This holistic engagement is vital for high performance, as engaged employees bring creativity, passion, and energy to their tasks. For instance, an employee in a psychologically safe organization might take more initiative and show a greater willingness to tackle complex projects, knowing that their efforts are valued and appreciated.

- **Higher Job Satisfaction**: Psychological safety contributes to job satisfaction, as individuals feel more supported and valued in a safe environment. Generally speaking, people feel that they will not be punished for making mistakes which has a positive impact on job satisfaction.[7] When individuals know they can express themselves without fear of retribution, they are more likely to feel fulfilled and satisfied with their work. For example, a customer service representative who feels supported by their team might enjoy their role more, as they can approach their manager with concerns or suggest improvements to processes without fear of being dismissed.

- **Motivation and Empowerment**: In psychologically safe environments, individuals feel that their opinions and contributions are valued, which fosters intrinsic motivation and a sense of empowerment. When employees see that their insights matter and that they have the freedom to make decisions, they are more likely to be motivated and committed to their work. For example, in a study of French and American engineering teams, those working in psychologically safe environments were more inclined to propose innovative solutions or improvements, knowing their ideas would be seriously considered. This empowerment contributes to a deeper commitment to their role and organization. This also leads to the creation of new team learning and team knowledge.[8]

SUPPORTING GROWTH AND LEARNING

Psychological safety fosters an environment conducive to growth and continuous learning by reducing the fear of failure and promoting knowledge sharing. In psychologically safe workplaces, individuals are more open to learning from their mistakes, seeking feedback, and sharing knowledge with colleagues.

- **Safe Learning Environment**: Psychological safety provides a supportive backdrop for learning and growth by reducing the fear of failure. When individuals feel safe, they are more likely to experiment, take risks, and learn from their mistakes. This type of environment enables individuals to continuously improve without the debilitating fear of making mistakes. For example, a young marketing professional who feels psychologically safe may be more willing to test new campaign ideas, knowing that even if the results aren't successful, they will gain valuable learning insights and won't be penalized.
- **Encouraging Knowledge Sharing**: Psychological safety promotes a culture of openness where individuals feel comfortable sharing information, insights, and constructive feedback. This openness is crucial for individual growth, as it enables employees to learn from one another and access diverse perspectives. For instance, in a psychologically safe team, a more experienced team member may feel comfortable mentoring a junior colleague, sharing lessons from past projects, and offering guidance without fearing that their advice will be perceived as criticism.

BENEFITS OF PSYCHOLOGICAL SAFETY FOR TEAMS

At the team level, the benefits of psychological safety include enhanced collaboration and communication, fostering innovation and creativity, mitigating burnout, and promoting team resilience.

ENHANCED COLLABORATION AND COMMUNICATION

Psychological safety significantly enhances collaboration and communication within teams. When team members feel safe to voice their ideas, raise concerns, and constructively disagree, the quality of teamwork improves, leading to better outcomes for the group and organization as a whole. In recent years, psychological safety has increasingly been understood as a team or group phenomenon, where it serves as a foundation for effective collaboration and collective intelligence.

- **Building Stronger Team Connections**: Psychological safety allows team members to establish trust, mutual respect, and a sense of connection. When teams operate in a psychologically safe environment, individuals feel valued and supported, which strengthens bonds within the team. Sports teams showing high psychological safety reported stronger bonds and higher levels of support among members.[9] In a corporate context, this can translate to teams where members feel comfortable relying on each other's expertise and working together toward common goals.

- **Encouraging Constructive Conflict**: Constructive conflict, or task conflict, is essential for team innovation and problem-solving. However, without psychological safety, team members may avoid conflict for fear of personal repercussions or damaging relationships. When psychological safety is present, team members feel comfortable engaging in debates and challenging ideas, leading to more thoughtful and robust solutions. If discussions become too heated or too personal, then performance will be affected. A key factor in ensuring that task conflict remains a productive activity is psychological safety. Bret Bradley and colleagues found that task conflict positively influences team performance when psychological safety is high, as it allows members to discuss differing perspectives openly and reach more innovative solutions. They described it memorably as "a context-shifting state that can alter the way conflict is received and managed in teams."[10]

- **Reduced Interpersonal Barriers**: Psychological safety reduces interpersonal barriers, allowing team members to go beyond departmental silos and collaborate across functions. This is particularly important regarding the relationships leaders form with team members.[11] When openness and cooperation are valued, team members are more willing to seek input from others and offer assistance, leading to a more cohesive team. For example, a marketing team that feels psychologically safe may regularly seek feedback from the sales department on campaign ideas, leading to marketing strategies that are better aligned with customer needs. This culture of open communication reduces misalignments between teams, fosters stronger relationships, and promotes organizational unity.

FOSTERING INNOVATION AND CREATIVITY

Psychological safety is a critical driver of innovation and creativity in teams. In a psychologically safe environment, team members feel empowered to experiment, take risks, and share unconventional ideas without fear of ridicule or failure. This freedom to innovate is essential for teams seeking to stay competitive in dynamic markets.

- **Encouraging Experimentation and Innovation**: Teams that feel psychologically safe are more likely to engage in experimentation and embrace failure as part of the learning process. Creativity thrives in environments where psychological safety exists, as team members feel free to explore new ideas without worrying about repercussions. In a tech startup, for example, a psychologically safe culture allows developers to test bold, new features, even if they might fail, fostering an innovative atmosphere that could lead to breakthrough products. This environment nurtures a growth mindset, where failure is viewed as an opportunity for improvement rather than a setback.[12]

  Research into R&D teams in the tech sector revealed that psychological safety enabled the team to experiment, innovate, and manage the stresses associated with their work. Not only was there an improvement in the performance of the R&D teams, but staff turnover was also reduced.[13] Working in a psychologically safe environment meant that people felt free to innovate and take risks. Team members openly discuss ideas for new products and challenge each other's assumptions, leading to a robust and creative development process.

- **Leveraging Diverse Perspectives**: A diverse team brings varied perspectives, which can lead to more creative solutions; however, without psychological safety, team members from different backgrounds may hesitate to share unique ideas. Psychological safety encourages individuals to contribute their insights regardless of their position, tenure, or background, fostering a culture of diversity and inclusion that is essential for innovation.[14] For example, in an international team with members from different cultural backgrounds, psychological safety enables team members to contribute ideas based on their cultural insights, creating a broader pool of ideas from which the team can draw.

- **Adapting to Change**: In times of rapid change, such as organizational restructuring or market shifts, teams that feel psychologically safe are better equipped to adapt. For example, during the COVID-19 pandemic, many teams had to transition quickly to remote working. Teams with high psychological safety were able to navigate this shift more effectively by openly discussing the challenges of remote working, sharing tips, and adapting their workflow together, resulting in a smoother transition. In a study looking at how teachers responded and reorganized themselves during the COVID-19 pandemic, they investigated the impact of psychological safety on learning, accountability (including rewards and discipline), professional culture, the principal, autonomy, infrastructure for teachers, collaboration, and decision-making. In every instance, they found that teams with high psychological safety had better outcomes on each of those five criteria.[15]

MITIGATING BURNOUT AND PROMOTING TEAM RESILIENCE

Psychological safety plays a protective role against burnout and fosters resilience within teams. In high-pressure environments, teams that feel safe can better manage stress, resolve conflicts constructively, and support one another, which contributes to overall team well-being.

- **Sustaining Team Well-Being**: Teams in psychologically safe environments experience lower levels of burnout because they feel supported and empowered. Task-focused climates help maintain vitality and mental health among team members. A psychologically safe team culture helps employees balance their workload, voice concerns about overwhelming tasks, and seek support when necessary, all of which reduce the risk of burnout.[16] A psychologically safe environment allows team members to express when they are feeling overwhelmed, enabling the team leader to redistribute tasks and provide additional resources as needed. Even in extreme circumstances, where someone has been humiliated at work, psychological safety, together with organizational support, mitigated the impact of potentially destructive experiences.[17]
- **Fostering Resilience**: In competitive sports, psychological safety allows team members to support each other through wins and losses. Achuthan Shanmugaratnam, a high-performance researcher at FIFA, and his colleagues highlighted that sports teams with high psychological safety report greater team resilience and cohesion.[18] Having the support of your colleagues is one of the most powerful ways of building resilience in a team, as it enables them to overcome the obstacles they face by utilizing all of the tenets and perspectives of each individual.
- **Improved Conflict Resolution**: Psychological safety and voice facilitate constructive conflict resolution, allowing teams to address issues openly and minimize long-term tensions. When

conflicts arise in psychologically safe teams, members feel comfortable discussing the issue without resorting to blame, which helps to prevent resentment and fosters team harmony.[19] This is particularly important in collaborative work environments where unresolved conflicts can hinder team performance. For instance, if a disagreement arises in a project team over deadlines or priorities, a psychologically safe environment enables team members to voice their concerns and work collaboratively to find a solution that satisfies everyone.

In recent years, psychological safety has increasingly been recognized as a team or group-level phenomenon where it finds its clearest expression. This shift in understanding reflects a positive development: it emphasizes the role of psychological safety in shaping the interactions and relationships that drive team success.

This team-centered approach aligns with research by Amy Edmondson and others, which highlights psychological safety as essential for effective team functioning. When teams collectively embrace psychological safety, members are more likely to support each other, uphold mutual accountability, and feel a shared sense of security.

BENEFITS OF PSYCHOLOGICAL SAFETY FOR ORGANIZATIONS

In recent years, psychological safety has increasingly been recognized as a critical factor not only at the individual and team levels but also as an organizational phenomenon. While the immediate effects of psychological safety may appear most evident in team dynamics, the impact of an organization-wide culture of psychological safety is profound.

BOOSTING ORGANIZATIONAL LEARNING AND KNOWLEDGE SHARING

Organizational learning and knowledge sharing are essential for any organization striving for continuous improvement and adaptation. Psychological safety fosters a culture where employees feel safe to share their insights, lessons from failures, and innovative ideas, which supports an environment of continuous learning.

- **Continuous Learning Culture**: Psychological safety enables an organization-wide learning culture by encouraging open discussion on what works and what doesn't. Psychological safety is critical in facilitating organizational learning, as it allows employees to reflect on their experiences without fear of blame or reprisal. In a psychologically safe organization, employees are encouraged to share lessons from unsuccessful projects, discuss challenges openly, and experiment with new approaches.
- **Encouraging Innovation at Scale**: Organizational-level studies, such as those conducted in 47 mid-sized organizations in Germany by Markus Baer and Michael Frese, indicate that psychological safety is closely linked to innovation and profitability.[20] In organizations where psychological safety is valued, employees are more willing to suggest improvements to existing processes, propose new ideas, and experiment with advanced techniques. This culture of innovation leads to increased competitiveness and profitability. Research in tech companies in Norway found that psychological safety contributed significantly to an organizations, innovation capability and to entrepreneurship. The researchers state that if an organization wants to have "radical innovation," they need to create an environment of psychological safety. Furthermore, they saw this as an organizational level intervention rather than at team or group level.[21]

- **Transactive Memory System (TMS)**: As Hendrik Wilhelm and his colleagues[22] point out, it's all very well talking about learning from failure, but that's easier said than done. We want people to respond to it positively, but it also creates a defensive reaction that makes people want to remove themselves from the situation. What they found in their research was that psychological safety supports the development of shared knowledge systems, such as Transactive Memory Systems (TMS), which enable teams to store information collectively and enhance coordination. Psychological safety, they found, strengthens TMS within teams, enabling better knowledge sharing and problem-solving. In an organization with a strong TMS, employees know who holds specific expertise and can easily access that knowledge. This collective intelligence allows for smoother project coordination and faster decision-making. For example, in a consulting firm with a well-established TMS, team members can quickly find experts within the organization to address client challenges, leading to more efficient and effective solutions.

ENHANCING EMPLOYEE RETENTION AND REDUCING TURNOVER

Employee retention is crucial for organizations seeking stability and consistency in their workforce. High turnover rates disrupt organizational cohesion, drain resources, and negatively impact team morale. Psychological safety is a key factor in enhancing employee retention by fostering a supportive and inclusive work environment.

- **Higher Retention Rates**: Organizations that prioritize psychological safety often enjoy lower turnover rates, as employees feel valued and supported in a psychologically safe environment. When employees know their voices are heard and respected, they are more likely to stay loyal to the organization. Research shows that psychological safety significantly reduces turnover by creating a culture of inclusion and belonging. For instance, an organization that encourages open dialogue and values employee input can retain top talent, as employees are less likely to feel alienated or undervalued. In a study involving 21 different teams in two healthcare organizations, fostering psychological safety helped retain skilled medical staff who feel valued and supported in their roles during the COVID-19 pandemic when they were under huge pressure. By promoting open communication and encouraging staff to voice concerns, the organization reduced turnover and built a loyal workforce. This stability contributed to higher-quality patient care and reduced recruitment costs, as experienced professionals were more likely to stay with the organization long-term.[23]

- **Attracting Top Talent**: As more employees prioritize mental health and well-being, organizations with a strong commitment to psychological safety become attractive employers. Job seekers increasingly look for workplaces that foster inclusivity, respect, and well-being, making psychological safety a competitive advantage in talent acquisition. For example, a technology company that promotes psychological safety in its recruitment campaigns may attract skilled candidates who value a supportive and innovative workplace. This not only strengthens the organization's talent pool but also enhances its employer brand in the industry.

IMPROVING BUSINESS PERFORMANCE AND PROFITABILITY

Psychological safety has a direct impact on business performance and profitability. By enabling employees to collaborate effectively, make decisions confidently, and contribute their best ideas, psychological safety drives productivity and operational efficiency.

- **Increased Productivity and Efficiency**: A psychologically safe environment encourages employees to take initiative and make decisions that drive productivity and efficiency.[24] This is due to employees feeling confident that they can voice concerns or propose solutions without fear of retribution, leading to enhanced collaboration and streamlined processes. For example, in a manufacturing company, employees might identify bottlenecks on the production line and suggest improvements, leading to reduced downtime and increased output.

- **Direct Impact on Financial Metrics**: Psychological safety at an organizational level is correlated with increased profitability.[25] When employees are encouraged to innovate and improve processes, the organization benefits from new revenue streams, cost savings, and increased efficiency. For instance, a financial services company that fosters psychological safety may empower its teams to develop and implement new investment products, resulting in higher profits and a stronger market position.

- **Future-Proofing the Organization**: In a rapidly changing market, organizations that foster psychological safety are better positioned to withstand disruptions. Psychological safety enables organizations to quickly mobilize resources, adapt to new challenges, and leverage the collective expertise of their workforce. This adaptability is crucial for long-term survival and growth. For example, during the COVID-19 pandemic, organizations with a culture of psychological safety were better equipped to transition to remote work, as employees felt comfortable discussing not just their work-related challenges but the emotional ones too.[26] It is also important to understand that the changes in the way people worked meant that approaches to maintaining psychological safety needed to be adapted—something that is discussed in Chapter 9.[27]This proactive approach helped these organizations remain resilient and maintain business continuity.

CONCLUSION

While psychological safety is often discussed as a team-level or individual-level concept, there is growing recognition of its importance at the organizational level. When psychological safety is embedded in an organization's culture, it fosters consistency in values, behaviors, and expectations across all teams and departments. This consistency promotes a cohesive work environment where psychological safety is a shared value, rather than a variable that depends on individual managers or teams.

By embracing psychological safety as a guiding principle in the way people conduct themselves, organizations can create a culture grounded in openness, trust, and mutual respect. This approach establishes an expectation that these values are woven into daily interactions, shaping a supportive environment where everyone feels safe to contribute. This unified approach ensures that psychological safety is not limited to isolated teams but is woven into the organization's fabric, benefiting everyone. For example, in a large healthcare organization, a commitment to psychological safety might be reflected in training programs, leadership expectations, and communication channels across all departments. This organization-wide approach not only supports high-quality patient care but also enhances employee well-being and retention.

The benefits of psychological safety at the organizational level are vast, contributing to enhanced learning, innovation, employee retention, and overall business performance. By embracing psychological safety as an organizational phenomenon, organizations can create a culture that prioritizes openness, trust, and continuous improvement. This culture not only supports individual and team success but also positions the organization for long-term growth and resilience in a competitive landscape. For organizations aiming to stay agile and innovative, investing in psychological safety is a strategic decision that fosters sustainable success and strengthens their foundation for future challenges.

KEY POINTS

Psychological safety doesn't simply emerge on its own. It doesn't arrive fully formed, nor does it spontaneously blossom in any given workplace. Rather, psychological safety is a product of deliberate actions, intentional choices, and consistent behaviors displayed by leaders and employees alike. It's a culture that is built over time, layer by layer, through policies, values, and ways of working that foster trust, openness, and respect.

Yet, as essential as it is, psychological safety is fragile. It can be meticulously crafted and nurtured over years, yet it takes far less time to be eroded, as the Boeing case study in Chapter 9 reveals. Just as safety is built through consistent, intentional acts, it can also be undone by a shift in leadership style, a lack of transparency, or even the absence of basic communication and trust. In this way, psychological safety is dynamic; it requires sustained commitment and reinforcement across all levels of the organization to truly thrive.

Creating psychological safety in an organization is much like cultivating a garden. Just as a garden requires the right combination of seeds, soil, water, and sunlight to flourish, psychological safety depends on nurturing various practices and values that create a supportive environment. Each "seed" you plant—whether it's encouraging open communication, establishing trust, or fostering a culture where mistakes are seen as learning opportunities—plays a role in cultivating an atmosphere where people feel safe to speak up, contribute, and learn from each other. And just like a garden, these elements don't thrive overnight; they require consistent care, attention, and sometimes a bit of adjustment based on what you observe along the way.

As any gardener will tell you, in a garden, not every plant will grow at the same rate, nor does every plant need the exact same conditions. Similarly, in an organization, some elements of psychological safety might take root faster than others. Perhaps open communication starts to flourish first, while inclusivity and trust take more time. That's okay. By tending to each area, you allow the overall culture to gradually become more resilient and supportive. The garden may not be perfect at every moment, and some parts might need extra care during challenging times. But with sustained effort and attention, a thriving, interconnected environment emerges, where individuals feel more at ease to engage, teams collaborate more effectively, and the organization as a whole becomes stronger and more adaptable.

And, of course, much like a garden, psychological safety offers both immediate and long-term rewards. There's joy and satisfaction in creating the environment itself, as you start to see openness, trust, and collaboration grow. Then there are the enduring benefits: the resilience, well-being, and success that a safe and nurturing culture can yield. To enjoy these you need to invest in the process and commit to cultivating it over time. In doing so, you create a space that doesn't just look good from the outside but truly nurtures and supports all who are part of it.

Think of it as a living system that benefits from continuous nurturing. Every interaction, every open conversation, and every small effort to listen or encourage can help the seeds of psychological safety grow a little stronger.

GLOSSARY

Well-being. A state of feeling healthy, happy, and fulfilled. Well-being includes physical health, mental and emotional balance, positive relationships, and a sense of purpose or satisfaction in life. It's about thriving, not just surviving, and can be influenced by personal habits, social connections, and environmental factors.

Transactive Memory Systems. The way groups share and manage knowledge. Everyone knows whom to ask for what. This makes it easier to work together, solve problems, and make decisions by combining everyone's strengths and knowledge.

Organizational learning. The process by which organizations improve and evolve by acquiring, sharing, and applying knowledge over time. The processes and the climate that are created enable individuals and teams to reflect on past experiences, including both successes and mistakes, and adapt to new challenges.

NOTES

1 Shanmugaratnam, A., McLaren, C.D., Schertzinger, M. & Bruner, M.W. (2024). Exploring the relationship between coach-initiated motivational climate and athlete well-being, resilience, and psychological safety in competitive sport teams. *International Journal of Sports Science & Coaching*, p. 17479541241278602.

2 Castaldelli-Maia, J.M., Gallinaro, J., Gde, M.E., Falcão, R.S. et al. (2019). Mental health symptoms and disorders in elite athletes: a systematic review on cultural influences and barriers to athletes seeking treatment. *BrJ Sports Med*, *53*, pp. 707–721.

3 Leroy, H., Dierynck, B., Anseel, F., Simons, T., Halbesleben, J.R., McCaughey, D., Savage, G.T., & Sels, L. (2012). Behavioral integrity for safety, priority of safety, psychological safety, and patient safety: a team-level study. *Journal of Applied Psychology*, *97*(6), p. 1273.

4 Shanmugaratnam, A., McLaren, C.D., Schertzinger, M. & Bruner, M.W. (2024). Exploring the relationship between coach-initiated motivational climate and athlete well-being, resilience, and psychological safety in competitive sport teams. *International Journal of Sports Science & Coaching*, p. 17479541241278602.

5 Baguio, C.A. & Heggem, E. (2021). What strengthens and weakens psychological safety in sales teams under Covid-19 and sudden virtuality? (Master's Thesis, Handelshøyskolen BI).

6 Kahn, W.A. (1990). Psychological conditions of personal engagement and disengagement at work. *Academy of Management Journal*, *33*(4), pp. 692–724.

7 Ahmad, Ifzal, & Waheed, Ali Umrani (2019). The impact of ethical leadership style on job satisfaction: Mediating role of perception of Green HRM and psychological safety. *Leadership & Organization Development Journal*, 40(5), p. 534–547.

8 Cauwelier, P., Vincent, M.R., & Bennet, A. (2019). The influence of team psychological safety on team knowledge creation: A study with French and American engineering teams. *Journal of Knowledge Management*, *23*(6), 1157–1175. DOI:https://doi.org/10.1108/JKM-07-2018-0420

9 Shanmugaratnam, A., McLaren, C.D., Schertzinger, M. & Bruner, M.W. (2024). Exploring the relationship between coach-initiated motivational climate and athlete well-being, resilience, and psychological safety in competitive sport teams. *International Journal of Sports Science & Coaching*, p. 17479541241278602.

10 Bradley, B.H., Postlethwaite, B.E., Klotz, A.C., Hamdani, M.R., & Brown, K.G. (2012). Reaping the benefits of task conflict in teams: The critical role of team psychological safety climate. *Journal of Applied Psychology*, *97*(1), p. 151.

11 Carmeli, A., Brueller, D., & Dutton, J.E. (2009). Learning behaviors in the workplace: The role of high-quality interpersonal relationships and psychological safety. Systems Research and Behavioral Science: *The Official Journal of the International Federation for Systems Research*, *26*(1), pp. 81–98.

12 Frazier, M.L., Fainshmidt, S., Klinger, R.L., Pezeshkan, A., & Vracheva, V. (2017). Psychological safety: A meta-analytic review and extension. *Personnel Psychology*, *70*(1), 113–165.

13 Chandrasekaran, A. & Mishra, A. (2012). Task design, team context, and psychological safety: An empirical analysis of R&D projects in high technology organizations. *Production and Operations Management*, *21*(6), pp. 977–996.

14 Bresman, H. & Edmondson, A.C. (2022). Exploring the relationship between team diversity, psychological safety, and team performance: Evidence from pharmaceutical drug development. *Harvard Business Review*, pp. 1–11.

15 Weiner, J., Francois, C., Stone-Johnson, C., and Childs, J. (2021, January). Keep safe, keep learning: principals' role in creating psychological safety and organizational learning during the COVID-19 pandemic. In *Frontiers in Education* (Vol. 5, p. 618483). Frontiers Media SA.

16 Ntoumanis, N., Dølven, S., Barkoukis, V., Boardley, I.D., Hvidemose, J.S., Juhl, C.B., & Gucciardi, D.F. (2024). Psychosocial predictors of

doping intentions and use in sport and exercise: a systematic review and meta-analysis. *British Journal of Sports Medicine, 58*(19), pp. 1145–1156.

17 Appelbaum, Nital P., Santen, Sally A., Perera, Robert A., Rothstein, William, Hylton, Jordan B., Hemphill, & Robin R. (2022). Influence of Psychological Safety and Organizational Support on the Impact of Humiliation on Trainee Well-Being. Journal of Patient Safety *18*(4): p 370–375. DOI: 10.1097/PTS.0000000000000927

18 Shanmugaratnam, A., McLaren, C.D., Schertzinger, M. & Bruner, M.W. (2024). Exploring the relationship between coach-initiated motivational climate and athlete well-being, resilience, and psychological safety in competitive sport teams. *International Journal of Sports Science & Coaching*, p. 17479541241278602.

19 Erkutlu, H. & Chafra, J. (2015). The mediating roles of psychological safety and employee voice on the relationship between conflict management styles and organizational identification. American *Journal of Business, 30*(1), pp. 72–91.

20 Baer, M. & Frese, M. (2003). Innovation is not enough: climates for initiative and psychological safety, process innovations, and firm performance. *Journal of Organizational Behavior, 24*(1), pp. 45–68.

21 Andersson, M., Moen, O., & Brett, P.O. (2020). The organizational climate for psychological safety: Associations with SMEs' innovation capabilities and innovation performance. *Journal of Engineering and Technology Management, 55,* p. 101554.

22 Wilhelm, H., Richter, A.W., & Semrau, T. (2019). Employee Learning from Failure: A Team-as-Resource Perspective. *Organization Science (Providence, R.I.), 30*(4), pp. 694–714.

23 Hebles, M., Trincado-Munoz, F., & Ortega, K. (2022). Stress and turnover intentions within healthcare teams: The mediating role of psychological safety and the moderating effect of COVID-19 worry and supervisor support. *Frontiers in Psychology, 12,* 758438.

24 Newman, A., Donohue, R., & Eva, N. (2017). Psychological safety: A systematic review of the literature. *Human Resource Management Review*, 27(3), 521–535.

25 Baer, M. & Frese, M. (2003). Innovation is not enough: climates for initiative and psychological safety, process innovations, and firm performance. *Journal of Organizational Behavior* 24(1), pp. 45–68.

26 Lee, H. (2021). Changes in workplace practices during the COVID-19 pandemic: the roles of emotion, psychological safety and organizational support. *Journal of Organizational Effectiveness: People and Performance, 8*(1), pp. 97–128.

27 Tkalich, A., Šmite, D., Andersen, N.H., & Moe, N.B. (2022). What happens to psychological safety when going remote? *IEEE Software, 41*(1), pp. 113–122.

FURTHER READING

Edmondson, A.C., 2019. *The fearless organization: Creating psychological safety in the workplace for learning, innovation, and growth*. Wiley.

Frazier, M.L., Fainshmidt, S., Klinger, R.L., Pezeshkan, A. and Vracheva, V., 2017. Psychological safety: A meta-analytic review and extension. *Personnel Psychology, 70*(1), pp. 113–165.

Gallo, A., 2023. What is psychological safety. *Harvard Business Review*, p. 15.

Video: Rafael Chiuzi "The Case for Psychological Safety and Better Teams" (TEDx Talks) – https://www.youtube.com/watch?v=MO3k6eGEJ5w

4

HOW DOES PSYCHOLOGICAL SAFETY IN ORGANIZATIONS RELATE TO OTHER CONCEPTS?

INTRODUCTION

Take a look at these two scenarios:

1. An employee notices an inefficient process at work. They face a choice: speak up to their manager in the hope it will lead to positive change, or remain silent, deciding it's not worth the risk of potential criticism. This decision—to voice or to withhold insights—depends on multiple factors within the workplace, particularly the culture of communication and the perceived consequences of speaking out.

2. Now consider Kalim, a new employee at a fast-growing technology firm. Eager to make a positive impression yet cautious, he is unsure how his ideas might be received. In his first project meeting, Kalim proposes an alternative approach to a standard process. His team leader, Tola, listens attentively and encourages him to elaborate. Days later, when Kalim makes a mistake, Tola coaches rather than criticizes him, turning the situation into a learning opportunity. These interactions early in his new job help him settle quickly into the team.

DOI: 10.4324/9781003501855-5

The first example introduces the concept of *voice*: the choice to express ideas, opinions, or concerns, which is shaped by both individual motivation and the broader team climate. The second example demonstrates the role of trust and psychological safety, showing how a leader's supportive actions can make an employee feel secure enough to take risks without fear of judgment or reprisal. In Kalim's case, the trust he develops with his team leader allows him to contribute fully, while the psychological safety of his team creates a foundation for open, constructive communication.

In previous chapters, we explored what psychological safety is and its benefits to individuals, teams, and organizations. In this chapter, we dive deeper into psychological safety's connection with voice and trust, examining how these concepts intersect and differ.

WHAT IS EMPLOYEE VOICE?

THE ORIGINS OF VOICE: WHY SPEAK UP?

In 1970, economist Albert Hirschman introduced the concept of "Exit–Voice–Loyalty,"[1] describing how people respond to dissatisfaction. According to Hirschman, individuals facing problems have three options:

- **Exit**: Leave the situation or organization.
- **Voice**: Speak up to try to improve the situation.
- **Loyalty**: Stay and endure the problem without complaint.

Hirschman's model was used in fields like industrial relations, where voice meant joining forces and taking collective action to bring about change, such as through union activity.[2]

By the 1990s, the concept of voice evolved again and psychologists Jeffery LePine and Linn Van Dyne redefined it as a positive, voluntary behavior, where employees suggest improvements or share feedback—not out of dissatisfaction, but out of a desire to help the organization grow. This shift reframed voice as a proactive, constructive action rather than purely a reaction to dissatisfaction, and the way a manager behaves will impact the extent to which people speak up. It is easy to see the connections between voice and psychological safety.[3]

Today, voice is often seen as a way to identify problems, propose solutions, and drive positive change. It is also used to bring forward the experiences of marginalized groups, for example Asian American women.[4]

However, not all voice is positive or constructive, which brings us to the different forms of voice.

TYPES OF VOICE: CONSTRUCTIVE AND DESTRUCTIVE

Voice in the workplace is not a single behavior but rather a range of actions—some helpful, others harmful, each impacting the organization differently. Researchers have identified various types of voice behaviors, each with distinct motivations and consequences. For example, promotive or prohibitive voice, where the former involves speaking about suggestions for improvement and the latter warns about potential risks or concerns.[5]

Or types of voice relate to either challenging or supporting the status quo. This can be done in a positive (supportive voice, constructive voice) or negative way (defensive voice, destructive voice).[6]

Understanding these types of voice highlights that employee voice is complex, comprising both constructive and potentially harmful behaviors. The impact of these different types of voice on an organization varies depending on the context and the way voice is received and managed.

HOW DO PSYCHOLOGICAL SAFETY AND VOICE INTERACT?

A useful metaphor for the relationship between psychological safety and voice is to think of psychological safety as the soil that allows voice (the plant) to grow. Without a safe environment, employees may hesitate to speak up, even if they have valuable ideas or concerns. Psychological safety removes the fear of negative consequences, making it easier for people to contribute openly.

However, psychological safety alone doesn't guarantee that people will speak up.

Employees also need motivation, encouragement, and sometimes guidance on how to voice their ideas constructively. In other words, psychological safety makes voice possible, but each individual must still choose to use their voice.

While psychological safety and voice are related, they serve different functions. Psychological safety is a shared team or organizational climate, a sense that it's okay to take risks and be honest. Voice, on the other hand, is an individual action—a choice to speak up with an idea, feedback, or concern. Psychological safety provides the supportive environment, but it's up to each person to decide whether or not to use their voice.

In Table 4.1 I have provided a comprehensive framework that considers psychological safety (high versus low), voice activity (high versus low), and the nature of voice (positive versus negative).

This $2 \times 2 \times 2$ model considers the level of psychological safety, voice activity, and whether the nature of voice is constructive or destructive. By exploring these interactions, we can understand how voice manifests across different organizational climates.

1. Low Psychological Safety, Low Voice (Silenced Environment)

   - *Positive Voice*: Absent. Employees in this environment rarely speak up, and constructive suggestions or concerns are unlikely to surface due to fear of retaliation.
   - *Negative Voice*: Present as Passive Destructive Voice. Employees might express dissatisfaction or cynicism through passive-aggressive or subtle negative behaviors, such as deliberate silence, withdrawal, or nonverbal signs of frustration e.g., sighing, eye rolling, avoiding eye contact.

Table 4.1 *Framework of Psychological Safety versus Type of Voice Activity*

Psychological Safety	Voice Level	Positive Voice	Negative Voice	Impact
Low	Low (Silenced)	Absent. Employees rarely share constructive ideas due to fear of retaliation or ridicule.	Passive Destructive Voice. Passive dissatisfaction, withdrawal, or calculated silence.	Suppressed feedback leads to stagnation and unresolved issues. Hidden frustrations create an unhealthy, disengaged environment.
Low	High (Divisive)	Rare. Constructive ideas come from a few employees motivated by strong personal convictions.	Active Destructive Voice. Harsh criticism and frustration expressed openly.	Constructive input is overshadowed by divisive criticism, creating conflict and polarizing team dynamics without proper support.
High	Low (Supportive but Quiet)	Low but constructive. Employees speak up occasionally and maintain a positive, solution-focused tone.	Rare. Passive dissatisfaction may occur subtly without major disruption.	Stable but risks stagnation. Limited active input hinders adaptability and innovation over time.
High	High (Thriving)	High. Employees actively provide feedback, share ideas, and suggest improvements constructively.	Varied. Both passive and active destructive voice may occur if not carefully managed.	Generally positive, fostering innovation and engagement. Excessive criticism must be addressed to maintain a respectful, constructive environment.

- *Impact*: The organization may suffer from suppressed feedback, stagnation, and hidden frustrations that could escalate over time. Without open communication, issues remain unresolved, creating an unhealthy environment.

2. Low Psychological Safety, High Voice (Risky Outspokenness)

- *Positive Voice*: Rare. A few employees might still voice constructive concerns, but they take personal risks, often motivated by strong personal convictions or moral reasons.
- *Negative Voice*: High in the form of Active Destructive Voice. With low psychological safety, voice may manifest negatively as frustration and criticism, sometimes harshly or confrontationally.
- *Impact*: While some employees might persist in sharing constructive ideas, many may use their voice to criticize or disrupt rather than improve. Without a supportive environment, this voice can be divisive, possibly fostering resentment and conflict.

3. High Psychological Safety, Low Voice (Supportive but Quiet Environment)

- **Positive Voice**: Low but non-disruptive. In a psychologically safe environment, employees may not see a need to speak up if they are content with the status quo. However, when they do express opinions, they maintain a constructive tone.
- **Negative Voice**: Rare and generally passive. Psychological safety limits destructive voice, but some employees may still exhibit passive dissatisfaction or disengagement.
- *Impact*: While this environment is stable, it may become stagnant if voice remains consistently low. Limited active input might reduce adaptability and responsiveness over time.

4. High Psychological Safety, High Voice (Thriving or Risk-Prone Environment)

- *Positive Voice*: High. In a safe environment, employees are likely to engage actively in constructive behaviors, such as offering ideas for improvement and providing feedback on practices.
- *Negative Voice*: Varied, including both passive and active forms of destructive voice. Although high psychological safety encourages openness, it doesn't necessarily prevent negative voice. Employees might feel emboldened to criticize excessively.
- *Impact*: This environment is generally positive, with high levels of constructive input driving innovation and improvement. However, too much criticism, if not addressed, can hold things back. It's important to keep feedback respectful and focused on finding solutions to make sure the voice remains helpful and productive.

This framework illustrates that psychological safety alone is not sufficient to ensure voice will be constructive. Leaders and managers must foster a respectful, solution-focused culture and set clear expectations for giving feedback to prevent psychological safety from enabling harmful voice behaviors.

By establishing clear guidelines and expectations for communication, organizations can leverage high psychological safety to encourage productive voice while minimizing potential downsides.

In essence, psychological safety lays the foundation for open communication, but it is the organization's cultural norms and leadership practices that shape whether voice—when it does occur—will be constructive or destructive. This nuanced view recognizes that voice in organizations is a double-edged sword, capable of driving both improvement and disruption, depending on the context in which it is expressed.

Actions

To address each quadrant in the model—considering high and low levels of psychological safety and both positive and negative forms of voice—organizations can implement targeted strategies. Here's an overview of actions that leaders and managers can take to maximize constructive voice, reduce destructive voice, and improve psychological safety across all scenarios:

1. Low Psychological Safety, Low Voice (Silenced Environment)
   Actions: Build psychological safety by demonstrating openness to feedback and reducing fear of repercussions. Leaders should model vulnerability and accountability, admit their mistakes, and provide structured feedback mechanisms (e.g., anonymous surveys) to allow employees to voice concerns safely.

2. Low Psychological Safety, High Voice (Risky Outspokenness)
   Develop clear communication norms for respectful feedback and address fear of negative consequences. Cultural change efforts, such as team-building or conflict resolution workshops, can foster a more open environment. Establishing channels for critical concerns, like anonymous reporting, can also help employees voice issues without fear.

3. High Psychological Safety, Low Voice (Supportive but Quiet Environment)
   Actions: Encourage feedback by asking open-ended questions like, "What do you think could improve in our current process?" or "How do you feel about the changes we've made recently?" and acknowledging people's input to get them more involved. Setting goals for continuous improvement or using techniques that focus on what's working well can inspire employees to share ideas for small changes.

4. High Psychological Safety, High Voice (Thriving or Risk-Prone Environment)
   Actions: Establish norms for constructive feedback to prevent an overly critical voice. Training on effective communication and feedback can ensure that the voice remains productive. Leaders should monitor voice patterns and encourage

reflection and self-regulation, balancing positive and critical feedback in discussions.

Managing Both Positive and Negative Voice Across All Quadrants

To maintain a balance of constructive feedback and minimize destructive voice, organizations can adopt overarching strategies:

- **Set a Constructive Tone from the Top**: Leaders should model solution-oriented, respectful feedback.
- **Formalize Feedback Processes**: Encourage a positive voice while minimizing negative voice by using a framework where criticisms are paired with constructive suggestions.
- **Create Consequences for Destructive Behavior**: Address destructive voice directly to protect team morale and productivity.
- **Foster a Growth-Oriented Culture**: Emphasize learning from mistakes and viewing feedback as essential to development.
- **Balance Freedom with Responsibility**: Encourage free expression while promoting respectful, team-building communication.

By tailoring these strategies to each quadrant, organizations can foster an environment where voice is constructive, purposeful, and balanced. This approach allows psychological safety and voice to create a dynamic, responsive, and resilient workplace.

EXPLORING TRUST AND PSYCHOLOGICAL SAFETY: FOUNDATIONS FOR A COLLABORATIVE ENVIRONMENT

Trust is a well-established concept in the study of organizational behavior. In recent years, psychological safety has become a popular term in discussions about workplace culture and team dynamics.

However, upon examining my own collection of organizational psychology texts—a comprehensive selection authored by some of the world's leading experts—an interesting pattern emerges. Out of 20 relatively recent seminal books on the subject, only two make direct reference to psychological safety. By contrast, trust is a recurring theme, explicitly mentioned in 14 of these works.

This contrast raises a fascinating question: could psychological safety, a relatively recent addition to our vocabulary, be simply a modern expression of concepts that have long been associated with trust? Is psychological safety merely an evolution in the language we use to describe trust, similar to how "stress" gradually replaced "nerves" in our everyday vernacular?[7] It's worth exploring whether these two concepts represent distinct ideas or if they are, in essence, two ways of discussing the same fundamental experience in human interaction.

In organizational settings, trust is often defined as "a psychological state involving a willingness to be vulnerable to others based on positive expectations of their intentions or behaviors"[8] (Rousseau et al., 1998). This willingness to be vulnerable is a significant aspect of trust, as it involves relying on others in situations where their actions could potentially impact one's well-being or interests. Trust, therefore, is not something that can be demanded or coerced; rather, it must be cultivated over time through consistent actions, shared experiences, and demonstrated reliability, as the second scenario at the start of this chapter showed.

Trust manifests in various forms and at multiple levels within organizations. For instance, affect-based trust emerges from emotional bonds, where individuals trust each other due to mutual respect, shared feelings, or affection.[9] Meanwhile, swift trust develops quickly within temporary teams or project groups that must collaborate under time constraints to achieve specific goals.[10] These distinctions highlight that trust is not a one-size-fits-all concept but rather a multifaceted phenomenon that adapts to different interpersonal and organizational needs. As with voice, trust, perhaps surprisingly, isn't always a good thing.

Where there are high levels of trust in people, it can lead to workplace behaviors that are counter-productive and damaging, as Professor Ros Searle, the UK's leading expert researching trust, has revealed.[11] It is interesting to note that early perceptions of fairness serve as a shortcut for assessing trustworthiness, especially in new relationships.[12]

These themes emphasize that trust is both complex and dynamic, shaped by individual interactions, collective experiences, and organizational practices. The role of trust is particularly significant in environments where collaboration, learning, and innovation are prioritized, as it enables individuals to engage fully and confidently in their work.

OVERLAP BETWEEN TRUST AND PSYCHOLOGICAL SAFETY

Given their shared goals of reducing fear and fostering openness, trust and psychological safety often overlap in significant ways. Both contribute to creating environments where individuals feel free to take risks—whether by sharing an idea, admitting a mistake, or challenging the status quo. In practice, experiencing one without the other can be challenging, as trust and psychological safety often reinforce each other.

Both concepts provide a foundation for risk-taking. When individuals trust their colleagues, they are more likely to feel psychologically safe, reassured that their vulnerabilities will not be exploited. Conversely, in a psychologically safe environment, individuals are more inclined to trust one another because the norms encourage openness, respect, and mutual support.

Furthermore, both trust and psychological safety rely on positive interpersonal expectations. Trust involves believing that others will act with good intentions, while psychological safety provides the assurance that one can express themselves without fear of judgment. This shared foundation of respect and goodwill encourages people to engage productively and collaboratively.

DIFFERENCES BETWEEN TRUST AND PSYCHOLOGICAL SAFETY

Despite their similarities, trust and psychological safety have distinct differences, each uniquely shaping organizational behavior and culture.

One primary difference is in their focus and scope. Trust often functions as an interpersonal, one-to-one relationship—such as the trust between a manager and an employee. Psychological safety, however, is a group-level construct that reflects the collective sense of security within a team or organization. While trust may exist between specific individuals, psychological safety seeks to create a supportive environment that includes everyone.

Another distinction lies in purpose and application. Trust emphasizes interpersonal reliability and cooperation, whereas psychological safety fosters a culture that encourages learning, innovation, and experimentation. Trust is often selective—an individual might trust certain colleagues but not others—while psychological safety aims to ensure that all group members feel safe to contribute.

The role of leadership also varies between the two. In building trust, leaders model reliability, integrity, and competence. In fostering psychological safety, leaders cultivate openness, inclusivity, and responsiveness, ensuring that team norms support participation and respect diverse viewpoints.

Finally, mistakes and failures are addressed differently. Trust allows individuals to admit mistakes within close relationships, while psychological safety promotes an organizational culture where mistakes are seen as learning opportunities, free from blame or shame.

Understanding trust and psychological safety as complementary rather than competing concepts can help organizations build environments that maximize collaboration, learning, and performance. Together, trust and psychological safety form a foundation on which individuals and teams can thrive. They create settings where people feel empowered to take risks, share insights, and engage in constructive conflict—essential elements for innovation and growth.

To foster both trust and psychological safety, organizations can take proactive steps. Supportive leadership is crucial; leaders who model openness, acknowledge their mistakes, and value diverse perspectives set a tone for an inclusive, trust-filled environment. Transparent communication is equally important. When leaders and team members communicate openly and honestly, misunderstandings are minimized, trust is strengthened, and psychological safety is enhanced.

KEY POINTS

In this chapter, we explored two key concepts—*voice* and *trust*—that are closely linked to psychological safety. By examining these ideas, we can get a clearer understanding of how they intersect with psychological safety, each bringing unique contributions to the workplace environment. While psychological safety shares much in common with both voice and trust, it also possesses a distinct quality that must be appreciated, identified, and cultivated to be fully utilized.

Understanding the interplay between these concepts allows us to appreciate the unique role that psychological safety plays in the workplace. While trust builds the interpersonal foundation and voice provides the channel for expression, psychological safety creates a climate that binds these elements together, enabling teams to operate at their highest potential.

By nurturing trust and encouraging constructive voice within organizations, we not only support psychological safety but also enhance its impact.

Gaining an understanding of these interrelated concepts allows us to leverage the full power of psychological safety, maximizing its potential to drive positive change, collaboration, and sustained organizational success.

GLOSSARY

Voice. In the workplace voice is not a single behavior but rather a range of actions—some helpful, others harmful, each impacting the organization differently. Researchers have identified various types of voice behaviors, each with distinct motivations and consequences.

Trust. Trust is often defined as "a psychological state involving a willingness to be vulnerable to others based on positive expectations of their intentions or behaviors."[13] This willingness to be vulnerable is a significant aspect of trust, as it involves relying on others in situations where their actions could potentially impact one's well-being or interests. Trust is both complex and dynamic, shaped by individual interactions, collective experiences, and organizational practices.

NOTES

1 Hirschman, A.O. (1970). *Exit, Voice, and Loyalty: Responses to Decline in Firms, Organizations, and* States. Harvard University Press.
2 Freeman, R.B. & Medoff, J.L. (1979). The two faces of unionism. NATIONAL BUREAU OF ECONOMIC RESEARCH 1050 Massachusetts Avenue Cambridge MA 02138 June 1979.
3 LePine, J.A. & Van Dyne, L. (1998). Predicting voice behavior in work groups. *Journal of Applied Psychology*, 83(6), p. 853.
4 Liang, J.G. & Peters-Hawkins, A.L. (2017). "I am more than what I look like": Asian American women in public school administration. *Educational Administration Quarterly*, *53*(1), pp. 40–69.

5 Liang, J., Farh, C.I., & Farh, J.L. (2012). Psychological antecedents of promotive and prohibitive voice: A two-wave examination. *Academy of Management Journal, 55*(1), pp. 71–92.

6 Gorden, W.I. (1988). Range of employee voice. *Employee Responsibilities and Rights Journal, 1*, pp. 283–299.

7 From nerves to neuroses (12 June 2019). https://www.sciencemuseum.org.uk/objects-and-stories/medicine/nerves-neuroses#:~:text=Museum%20Group%20Collection-,The%20nervous%20breakdown,George%20III%20assured%20his%20court

8 Rousseau, D.M., Sitkin, S.B., Burt, R.S. & Camerer, C. (1998). Not so different after all: A cross-discipline view of trust. *Academy of Management Review, 23*(3), pp. 393–404.

9 McAllister, D.J. (1995). Affect- and cognition-based trust as foundations for interpersonal cooperation in organizations. *Academy of Management Journal*, 38(1), pp. 24–59.

10 Blomqvist, K. & Cook, K.S. (2018). Swift trust: State of the art and future research directions. In Searle, R.H., Nienaber, A.M.I., & Sitkin, S.B. eds., *The Routledge companion to trust*. Routledge.

11 Searle, R.H. and Rice, C. (2025). Trust, and high control: an exploratory study of Counterproductive Work Behaviour in a high security organization. *European Journal of Work and Organizational Psychology, 34*(3), pp. 392–402.

12 Lind, E.A. (2018). Trust and fairness. In Searle, R.H., Nienaber, A.M.I. & Sitkin, S.B. eds., *The Routledge Companion to Trust*. Routledge.

13 Rousseau, D.M., Sitkin, S.B., Burt, R.S., & Camerer, C. (1998). Not so different after all: A cross-discipline view of trust. *Academy of Management Review, 23*(3), pp. 393–404.

FURTHER READING

Kahn, W.A., 1990. Psychological conditions of personal engagement and disengagement at work. *Academy of Management Journal*, 33(4), pp. 692–724.

Liang, J., Farh, C.I.C. and Farh, J.L., 2012. Psychological antecedents of promotive and prohibitive voice: A two-wave examination. *Academy of Management Journal*, 55(1), pp. 71–92.

Rousseau, D.M., Sitkin, S.B., Burt, R.S. and Camerer, C., 1998. Not so different after all: A cross-discipline view of trust. *Academy of Management Review*, 23(3), pp. 393–404.

PART II
THE HUMAN ELEMENT

How leaders, teams, and individuals shape psychological safety.

This part focuses on personal responsibility and interpersonal dynamics—highlighting how leadership behaviour, team norms, and inclusive practices drive (or erode) safety at work.

DOI: 10.4324/9781003501855-6

5

HOW DO LEADERS IMPACT PSYCHOLOGICAL SAFETY?

INTRODUCTION

This chapter explores the role of leadership in creating psychologically safe working environments and how they can go about creating unsafe, even toxic workplaces. I will examine leadership authority, groupthink, and the power of personalities in creating toxic working environments, also known as the Dark Triad.

THE QUIET FORCE OF AUTHORITY

According to surveys, the vast majority of psychologists, students, and laypeople believe that individuals could never be persuaded to carry out unethical acts causing deliberate harm to others. This overwhelming consensus is reassuring. People believe that morality is such an intrinsic part of human nature that it's almost impossible to imagine setting out to inflict pain on someone we have only just met and for no reason at all. Psychiatrists even predicted that only a psychologically flawed few—perhaps one in a thousand—would deliberately and voluntarily inflict pain on another human being just because somebody told them to do so.

These assumptions, however, were tested in the psychology laboratory of a university in the early 1960s, where ordinary people

DOI: 10.4324/9781003501855-7

sat down for what they thought was a simple experiment on memory and learning. The study, as well as the survey that preceded it, which I have just summarized, was carried out by the renowned psychology professor Stanley Milgram.

The setting was unremarkable: a plain room, a rather large, imposing machine with labeled switches, and an authoritative figure in a white lab coat calmly issuing instructions. Yet, over the course of an hour, something extraordinary unfolded—something that totally contradicted the survey results and would forever change our understanding of how we respond to authority.

The participants, referred to as "teachers," were tasked with delivering increasingly severe electric shocks to a "learner" every time they made a mistake in recalling word pairs. The learner, seated in another room and strapped to a device, was not truly being shocked—he was an actor, but the teacher did not know this. The experimenter, an imposing and confident figure, prompted the teacher to continue administering shocks, even when the learner cried out in pain, begged for the experiment to stop, and then fell disturbingly silent. The shock levels ranged from mild jolts to a terrifying 450 volts, labeled with ominous warnings such as "Danger: Severe Shock."

The actual results totally contradicted the early assumptions reached in the survey. In the baseline condition, with the learner pleading for the teacher to stop before falling into silence, 65% of participants delivered the maximum shock. Many participants clearly didn't feel comfortable to continue administering the shocks because they could be seen trembling, sweating, and showing other visible signs of distress. Yet, they continued. When asked later why they did not stop, their answers were disconcerting in their simplicity: "I was just following orders."

Milgram's groundbreaking experiments revealed a disturbing truth: authority figures exert immense power over our actions, often more than we realize or are willing to admit. For all our belief in personal autonomy, we are deeply susceptible to the influence of those we perceive as legitimate authorities, which plays out anywhere hierarchical structures exist—boardrooms, classrooms, military bases, and hospitals. And its implications for leadership and psychological safety are profound.

It's important to point out that no one was physically coerced into administering the shocks. Instead, this study revealed the subtle psychological mechanisms of social order. From a young age, we are taught to respect and obey authority figures—parents, teachers, clergy, police officers. In our view of the world, authority is synonymous with legitimacy and competence.

In Milgram's laboratory, the experimenter did not shout, threaten, or physically force participants to comply. Instead, he relied on calm, firm instructions: "The experiment requires that you continue." "You have no other choice." These statements, delivered with quiet confidence, were enough to override the participants' moral concerns. The authority figure's demeanor (confident and sure), dress (the lab coat), and the scientific setting (a laboratory at a prestigious university) all contributed to creating an aura of respectability and credibility that most participants found difficult to challenge.

The important observation was the participants' tendency to deflect responsibility for their actions. Many saw themselves as instruments of the experimenter's will rather than autonomous beings. This phenomenon, which Milgram called the "agentic state," allowed them to reconcile their actions with their conscience. They were not "hurting" the learner, they rationalized; they were merely carrying out orders. They were not responsible for the pain being inflicted—it was the investigator who was the cause.

This disconnect between self-perception and actual behavior is not unique to the laboratory. In organizations, employees often conform to the expectations of managers and leaders, even when those expectations conflict with personal values. Nor is it just about those who actively carry out the instructions; it encompasses more subtle behaviors, such as staying silent during unethical decisions or withholding feedback that might challenge authority. The fear of repercussions, whether explicit or implicit, can create a culture where obedience trumps integrity.

AUTHORITY AND PSYCHOLOGICAL SAFETY

Milgram's experiments hold important lessons for leaders who wish to create environments where people feel safe to speak up and act according to their values. The first step is to recognize that authority has not only power but also responsibility. Leaders must be aware of how their words, actions, and conduct influence those around them. A simple directive can carry disproportionate weight when it comes from someone in a position of power.

Leaders who foster psychological safety encourage employees to challenge assumptions, voice dissenting opinions, and hold one another accountable. On the leader's part, this requires humility, empathy, and a willingness to be questioned. It also means we should not expect individuals to act autonomously; we need to have systems that distribute authority and empower.

While the focus of attention is typically on the people who followed through on the instructions they were given, it is just as important, if not more so, to look at the conditions that prevailed when people chose to disobey. In one of the many variations of the experiment, when participants were allowed to choose the shock level, the majority opted for the lowest setting, which shows that people are not inherently cruel but are often influenced by situational factors.

Other variations revealed the conditions that prevailed when people resisted authority. The closer participants were to the consequences of their actions, such as physically interacting with the victim or witnessing their distress firsthand, the more likely they were to disobey. This highlights the role of empathy in fostering resistance to unethical directives.

Conversely, when the authority figure was physically distant or perceived as less legitimate, participants felt less compelled to comply. Observing peers defy authority was another powerful factor, as it showed that dissent was a possibility.

Contradictory commands from authority figures also undermined obedience by creating confusion, reducing the perceived legitimacy of authority, and prompting participants to act independently.

These insights emphasize key principles for fostering psychological safety in organizations. Leaders can create environments where individuals feel secure in speaking up by reducing emotional and hierarchical distance, encouraging open dialogue, and providing clear expectations. Empathy-driven leadership, peer support, and clear, consistent communication play critical roles in helping individuals reclaim their sense of agency, align their actions with shared values, and resist harmful pressures.

AUTHORITY'S DOUBLE-EDGED SWORD

Authority itself is not inherently good or bad; its value depends on how it is wielded. In Milgram's experiments, authority figures used their position to bring about harmful actions. But authority can also be a force for good, guiding people toward shared goals and ethical outcomes. The challenge for leaders is to use their influence responsibly, balancing the need for structure and direction with respect for individual autonomy.

By acknowledging the psychological pressures that authority can place on team members and followers, leaders can help their teams navigate these challenges with greater awareness and resilience.

However, the use of authority in leadership becomes even more complex when decisions are made collectively. While leaders have the ability to steer their teams toward ethical and effective outcomes, their influence can sometimes hinder open communication and critical thinking, resulting in flawed decisions.

Table 5.1 *Summary Table of Key Lessons for Psychological Safety From Those Who Disobeyed Authority*

Condition of disobedience	Explanation	Application for psychological safety
Closeness to victim	Empathy increased when participants witnessed or physically interacted with the victim, leading to more disobedience.	Foster empathy by reducing emotional distance between decisions and their consequences.
Distance from authority	Authority felt less compelling when the experimenter was absent, leading to higher disobedience rates.	Reduce overbearing authority; encourage approachable and collaborative leadership.
Peer influence	Observing peers defy authority normalized dissent and empowered participants to resist.	Encourage collective accountability and model open dialogue within teams.
Contradictory commands	Conflicting instructions from authority figures created confusion, prompting participants to act independently.	Be consistent with your values and create space for open discussion if anyone feels the values are being ignored.
Agentic state versus personal agency	Participants who obeyed often relinquished responsibility to the authority figure. Disobedience arose when participants reclaimed agency.	Empower individuals to take ownership of decisions and highlight their autonomy.

GROUPTHINK

How often have you heard yourself or others say "How could they have been so stupid?" when commenting on awful, sometimes disastrous decisions made by leaders in government organizations? The experience and abilities of those involved only serve to make their decisions even more inexplicable. It was a question like this that led Irving Janis, the noted psychologist and academic, to explore it in greater depth.

Irving Janis developed his theory of groupthink to understand why intelligent and competent groups often make flawed decisions, especially in high-stakes situations. His interest was sparked by historical policy failures, including the destruction of the United States Pacific Fleet at Pearl Harbor in 1941, the disastrous Bay of Pigs Invasion of Cuba in 1961, and the Watergate cover-up, which eventually led to President Richard Nixon's resignation in 1974. For Janis, the question was not about individual incompetence but about group dynamics that could systematically undermine rational decision-making. These episodes highlighted how cohesive, high-level advisory groups could fall into patterns of poor decision-making by prioritizing unity and consensus over critical thinking and dissent.

Janis was also deeply influenced by his background in psychology, particularly research on cognitive dissonance and conformity. He sought to connect these psychological concepts to the political and organizational contexts, providing a framework for understanding how social and cognitive biases affect group decision-making. The context of his work, during the Cold War, heightened the stakes of decision-making, as small groups of policymakers were making decisions with potentially catastrophic global consequences. But he wasn't just interested in diagnosing these failures; he wanted to offer practical solutions, helping leaders and organizations adopt practices that encourage critical thinking and avoid the pitfalls of groupthink.

PRINCIPAL METHODS OF ANALYSIS

Janis's analysis of groupthink was primarily qualitative, involving detailed case studies of historical decision-making failures and successes. He examined major US Government decisions, such as the Bay of Pigs invasion and the escalation of the Korean War. For each case, he systematically analyzed meeting transcripts, memoirs, and historical records to identify patterns of behavior and decision-making within the groups involved (for Watergate, he, of course, had the transcripts of the notorious recordings that had been made). By comparing these cases, he identified a recurring set of symptoms of something he called groupthink, being inspired by George Orwell's use in his novel 1984 of the terms "doublethink" and "crimethink."

Usefully, Janis employed a comparative approach, contrasting cases of poor decision-making with those where groups successfully avoided groupthink. The Bay of Pigs failure, for example, was contrasted with the Cuban Missile Crisis, where President Kennedy and his team employed strategies like encouraging open debate and consulting outside experts, which led to a more successful outcome. Through these comparisons, Janis was able to isolate the conditions that foster groupthink and those that mitigate it. His methods combined psychological theory with real-world application, bridging the gap between social psychology and political science to provide actionable insights into decision-making processes that have been used more widely beyond government bodies.

SYMPTOMS OF GROUPTHINK

Groupthink is defined as "a deterioration of mental efficiency, reality, testing, and moral judgements that results from in group pressures" [1](He also identified eight symptoms of groupthink divided into three types.

Type I: Overestimations of the group's power and morality

1. **Illusion of Invulnerability**: Group members share a strong sense of optimism that encourages risk-taking and creates a sense that the group cannot fail.
2. **Belief in Inherent Morality of the Group**: The group members believe their actions are morally superior, leading them to ignore ethical concerns.

Type II: Closed-mindedness

3. **Collective Rationalization**: Members discount warnings and negative feedback, rationalizing decisions to reinforce group views and avoid rethinking their stance.

4. **Stereotyping of Enemy Leaders**: The enemy leaders are seen as evil, weak, or incapable, and so there is little point in negotiating with them, which further justifies the group's stance and actions.

Type III: Pressures toward uniformity

5. **Self-Censorship**: Individuals with doubts or concerns tend to keep them to themselves to avoid disrupting group harmony. They start to believe that their doubts are not important.

6. **Illusion of Unanimity**: The lack of dissenting opinions is taken as evidence of total agreement, which is bolstered by self-censorship. Silence is taken as agreement with proposals.

7. **Direct Pressure on Dissenters**: Members who express doubts or pose questions are pressured to conform to the group's consensus. It can be presented as an issue of loyalty to the leader and to the group itself.

8. **Mindguards**: Some members act as self-appointed gatekeepers, shielding the group from information or viewpoints that might disrupt consensus.

THE PERFECT FAILURE: BAY OF PIGS INVASION

Janis referred to the incidents he examined as "fiascoes," and of these he called the Bay of Pigs invasion the "Perfect Failure."

Just two days after the inauguration of President John F. Kennedy in January 1961, his administration was being briefed by senior CIA officials on a daring plan to invade Cuba and overthrow its president, Fidel Castro. The plan had been conceived by the CIA during the previous administration, without President Eisenhower's knowledge, and was being pitched to those now in charge. Events moved very swiftly and by April 17, 1961, approximately 1,400 Cuban exiles landed on the Bay of Pigs in Cuba as an invading army. Within days, the whole exercise had descended into a military and political humiliation.

It is one of the clearest examples of how a group of intelligent, experienced individuals can make a disastrously poor decision when groupthink takes hold. Irving Janis's analysis of this "fiasco" identified several symptoms that contributed to the failure, all rooted in how President Kennedy's advisory team worked—or failed to work—together.

Overconfidence and Illusions of Success

The group fell victim to an illusion of invulnerability, where members believed the plan was destined to succeed simply because they were all in agreement and confident in their collective judgment. The risky nature of the invasion was brushed aside with an almost magical faith that luck would be on their side. This overconfidence blinded them to the very real challenges and risks of the operation.

False Consensus and Avoiding Conflict

Another problem was the illusion of unanimity—everyone assumed the group was completely aligned because no one wanted to disrupt the apparent harmony. Instead of exploring differences of opinion, the group chose to focus on areas of agreement, avoiding hard questions that might disturb the peace. There was a collective desire to keep the atmosphere pleasant, even if that meant ignoring serious doubts about the plan's viability.

Suppressing Dissent

Many in the group suppressed their personal doubts. Even individuals who harbored strong reservations chose to remain silent, fearing they might annoy others or, worse, lose their peers' approval. Group members prioritized fitting in over speaking up, which led to an absence of meaningful debate.

The Role of "Mindguards"

Robert Kennedy, acting as a "mindguard," actively discouraged dissent. At a social event to celebrate his wife's birthday, he privately told Arthur Schlesinger, the Harvard historian and political advisor, who had concerns about the plan, to stop voicing his objections because the president had already made up his mind. His message was clear: it was time to support the decision, not question it. This intervention further cemented the group's unwillingness to address alternative perspectives.

Leadership Style and Group Pressures

Kennedy himself fostered an atmosphere that discouraged opposition, even unintentionally. While he asked questions in meetings, he often gave more prominence to those who supported the invasion, particularly CIA representatives. When objections arose, he would shift the conversation, signaling that disagreement wasn't welcome. This left others reluctant to challenge the plan. Janis elegantly described this as "Docility fostered by suave leadership".[2]

Seeking Approval from Outsiders

The group was also influenced by the desire to please "valuable" new members, particularly those who had served in the Eisenhower administration, like the CIA officials. These individuals carried significant weight, and their support for the invasion plan discouraged others from raising concerns. Their status as powerful insiders created an environment where their opinions were overly respected, further stifling debate.

Ultimately, Kennedy's inner circle sought consensus at the expense of gathering critical information, challenging assumptions, or engaging in meaningful debate. This led to overconfidence, complacency, and a failure to fully address the uncertainties and risks of the invasion. The result was one of the most famously disastrous decisions in modern history—a military operation so poorly conceived that it became a global symbol of failure.

It is a telling case study, the lessons of which have not been fully learned.

PREVENTING GROUPTHINK

Janis's analysis also led to a series of recommendations for preventing groupthink by fostering openness, encouraging diverse viewpoints, and minimizing the pressures to conform—all of which align closely with the principles of psychological safety.

1. Assign a Critical Evaluator

   Encouraging a critical evaluator to raise objections and challenge assumptions sends a clear message that dissent and constructive criticism are valued. This aligns with psychological safety by:

   - Creating an expectation that voicing concerns is not only allowed but also necessary.
   - Reducing fear of negative consequences for challenging group norms, as it normalizes dissent as part of the process.
   - Helping team members feel confident that their unique contributions will be respected, even if they contradict the majority.

2. Leader Impartiality

   When leaders avoid expressing strong preferences early in discussions, they create space for open inquiry and balanced debate. This approach promotes psychological safety by:

- Reducing the implicit pressure to agree with the leader's opinions, which can discourage dissent.
- Encouraging team members to share their honest thoughts without worrying about contradicting authority figures.
- Allowing diverse viewpoints to surface, fostering a sense of inclusion and respect for different perspectives.

3. Multiple Policy-Planning Groups
   Breaking larger teams into smaller, independent groups to explore the same issue reduces the fear of speaking out in large settings and prevents groupthink. This supports psychological safety by:

   - Giving individuals the opportunity to express their ideas in a smaller, less intimidating context.
   - Preventing the dominance of a single "in-group" or prevailing narrative, which might discourage alternative viewpoints.
   - Encouraging fresh perspectives by promoting cross-group dialogue and collaboration.

4. Subgroups for Feasibility Studies
   Dividing teams into smaller subgroups fosters psychological safety by:

   - Allowing individuals to express their views in a more intimate setting, reducing fear of judgment in larger groups.
   - Providing multiple forums for discussion, where differing opinions can be explored without the pressure of immediate group consensus.
   - Creating a structured process for reconciling differences, reinforcing the idea that diverse viewpoints are critical to success.

5. Discuss with Outside Associates
   Encouraging team members to seek external opinions fosters psychological safety by:

- Validating the importance of exploring diverse perspectives and viewpoints.
- Reducing internal group pressure by allowing individuals to step outside the group's dynamic and bring in fresh insights.
- Reinforcing the idea that disagreement and alternative ideas are valuable to the decision-making process.

6. Invite Outside Experts
Bringing in external experts to challenge assumptions reduces insularity and promotes psychological safety by:

- Demonstrating that differing viewpoints, even from outside the group, are welcomed and respected.
- Showing team members that the organization values critical thinking and is open to being challenged.
- Creating an environment where questioning is normalized, making internal members more comfortable voicing dissent.

7. Appoint a Devil's Advocate
The devil's advocate role formalizes the process of questioning assumptions and challenging majority opinions, supporting psychological safety by:

- Protecting dissenters from being singled out, as it institutionalizes dissent as part of the process.
- Encouraging team members to think critically, knowing that alternative perspectives are part of the group's culture.
- Reducing the fear of reprisal for expressing unpopular or contrary views.

8. Alternative Scenarios in Rival Situations
Exploring alternative scenarios and warning signals promotes psychological safety by:

- Encouraging proactive thinking and demonstrating that all contributions, even those highlighting risks, are important.

- Reducing the stigma around raising concerns or pointing out potential failures, as it is framed as an essential step in decision-making.
- Ensuring that team members see value in their perspectives, even when those perspectives focus on worst-case outcomes.

9. Hold a "Second-Chance" Meeting
   Revisiting decisions after an initial consensus reinforces psychological safety by:

   - Giving team members another opportunity to express concerns or share doubts, reducing the fear of missing a chance to speak up.
   - Normalizing reflection and re-evaluation, which shows that the group values thoroughness over rushing to agreement.
   - Encouraging individuals to raise issues without feeling like they are disrupting the process, as this step is intentionally built into the workflow.

Summary

Janis's recommendations align well with psychological safety because they explicitly aim to create an environment where open communication, dissent, and critical thinking are encouraged. By implementing these practices, leaders can ensure their teams feel safe to share ideas, challenge assumptions, and contribute to decisions without fear of judgment or repercussions. This fosters not only better decisions but also a more engaged, innovative, and resilient team culture.

WHAT PART DOES THE PERSONALITY OF THE LEADER PLAY IN PSYCHOLOGICAL SAFETY?

The personality of leaders profoundly influences the way they carry out their duties, shaping the environment they foster within their teams. In some workplaces, individuals thrive on bending rules, manipulating others, and pursuing self-interest above all else. These are not merely difficult colleagues or bosses—they may exemplify the Dark Triad of personality traits: Machiavellianism, Narcissism, and Psychopathy. While not always clinical disorders, these traits often manifest as destructive behaviors that damage workplace relationships and psychological safety.

THE DARK TRIAD IN LEADERSHIP

Each element of the Dark Triad contributes uniquely to workplace toxicity:

- **Machiavellianism**: Named after Niccolò Machiavelli, this trait is defined by strategic manipulation and deception. Machiavellians use others as tools to achieve their goals, often hiding their true motives behind a professional facade. Their long-term focus on personal gain often comes at the expense of ethical standards and coworkers' well-being.
- **Narcissism**: Narcissists crave admiration, possess an inflated sense of self-importance, and exhibit entitlement. In leadership, they often dominate discussions and dismiss others' contributions, prioritizing their image over organizational goals. Their hypersensitivity to criticism and lack of empathy further alienate team members.
- **Psychopathy**: Psychopaths exhibit impulsivity, emotional coldness, and a lack of remorse. They often thrive in high-pressure environments and may appear calm under stress. However, their disregard for others' rights and feelings leads to

exploitative, impulsive actions focused on immediate gratification rather than long-term benefits.

At first glance, individuals with Dark Triad traits may seem charismatic or highly competent, often rising to leadership roles. Their bold decisions and unflappable demeanor can initially inspire confidence. Yet beneath this exterior lies a toxic mix of manipulation, egotism, and emotional callousness. Over time, their behaviors erode trust, stifle collaboration, and leave behind demoralized employees and a damaged organizational culture.

THE IMPACT OF THE DARK TRIAD ON PSYCHOLOGICAL SAFETY

Recognizing and addressing the Dark Triad is essential for maintaining psychological safety—the shared belief that individuals can take risks, voice opinions, and admit mistakes without fear of humiliation or retaliation. Leaders with Dark Triad traits threaten this foundation in several ways:

- **Fear and Distrust**: Manipulative, self-serving behaviors foster an environment of suspicion and competition. Employees become guarded, unwilling to share ideas or collaborate openly.
- **Erosion of Morale**: Narcissists' dismissal of others' contributions and hypersensitivity to criticism demoralize teams, while psychopaths' exploitative actions heighten stress and create conflict.
- **High Turnover**: The toxic atmosphere created by Dark Triad leaders drives employees to leave, increasing turnover and reducing organizational stability.

Addressing the Dark Triad in the Workplace

Organizations can mitigate the influence of Dark Triad traits by implementing strategies to identify and manage individuals who exhibit these behaviors:

- **Better Hiring Practices**: Structured interviews and behavioral assessments can help screen for manipulative tendencies.
- **Leadership Development**: Ethical training and monitoring programs can limit opportunities for exploitative behavior.
- **Team-Based Decision-Making**: Group accountability reduces the ability of any single individual to dominate or manipulate.
- **Succession Planning**: Establishing clear pathways for leadership helps prevent individuals with toxic traits from gaining unchecked power.

By understanding the Dark Triad and its impact, organizations can take steps to protect workplace culture, improve psychological safety, and promote employee well-being.

SHIFTING FOCUS: THE LIGHT TRIAD

In contrast to the toxicity of the Dark Triad, the Light Triad offers a more hopeful perspective. Characterized by empathy, compassion, and cooperation, the Light Triad fosters meaningful relationships and strengthens the foundation of psychological safety. These traits act as a natural antidote to the harm caused by manipulative, egocentric behaviors, creating environments where trust, collaboration, and innovation thrive.

The Light Triad is strongly associated with Organizational Citizenship Behaviors (OCBs)—voluntary actions that go beyond job requirements to benefit teams and organizations. Examples include mentoring colleagues, resolving conflicts peacefully, and supporting team morale. OCBs are the social glue that holds organizations together, improving productivity and enhancing workplace culture.

Research links OCBs with traits such as pro-social orientation and empathy, which Light Triad individuals naturally exhibit. Their behaviors benefit the workplace in several ways:

- **Empathy and Compassion**: Light Triad individuals prioritize understanding others' needs, fostering mutual respect and support.
- **Cooperation and Forgiveness**: They emphasize collaboration and shared goals, avoiding grudges and ensuring conflicts do not derail progress.
- **Self-Awareness**: Mindful of how their actions affect others, Light Triad individuals align their behaviors with organizational values, maintaining harmony and morale.

The influence of the Light Triad extends across the organization not just in terms of psychological safety but also in the creation of an inclusive work culture where people feel valued and motivated. It is also associated with reduced counterproductive work behaviors.

Developing the Light Triad versus Addressing the Dark Triad

We can too easily become so focused on the damage that some individuals can cause that we forget about developing our capabilities to create a work environment where people are engaged, feel psychologically safe, and as a result, are more productive. We also need to recognize that the Light Triad and Dark Triad represent opposite ends of the personality spectrum, requiring distinct approaches in the workplace, where the Light Triad needs to be developed and the Dark Triad needs to be contained. Some ways of doing this are outlined in Table 5.2 where they can be seen that strengthening and containing are two different sets of strategies.

Table 5.2 *Ways to develop the Light Triad and Address the Dark Triad*

Aspect	Developing the Light Triad	Addressing the Dark Triad
Organizational culture	• Builds inclusivity, trust, and pro-social behaviors. • Rewards collaboration, openness, and creativity.	• Clear policies for bullying, dishonesty, and manipulation. • Protects victims of toxicity.
Hiring strategies	• Prioritizes hiring individuals with strong emotional intelligence and ethical alignment. • Behavioral-based interviews to assess pro-social traits.	• Uses screening tools to identify manipulative tendencies. • Avoids rewarding charisma without ethical substance.
Performance management	• Uses screening tools to identify manipulative tendencies. • Avoids rewarding charisma without ethical substance.	• Focus on identifying toxic behaviors even in high performers, ensuring negative behaviors don't undermine culture.
Leadership development	• Encourage servant leadership and ethical decision-making. • Promote psychological safety and collaboration.	• Identify development needs where people are creating unsafe environments.
Learning and development approaches	• Growth-focused training (e.g., empathy workshops, mindfulness training, ethical leadership programs).	• Preventative training (e.g., boundary-setting, conflict management, leadership oversight programs).
Accountability mechanisms	• Positive reinforcement through recognition programs and feedback systems. • Focuses on both results and behaviors.	• Strict monitoring with enforced consequences for harmful actions. • Ensures behaviors align with organizational values.

By recognizing both the Dark Triad and Light Triad, we have a better appreciation of the actions we can take and the type of working environment we can seek to foster.

CASE STUDY: THE IRAQ WAR AND THE CHILCOT INQUIRY—A CASE STUDY IN PSYCHOLOGICAL SAFETY, GROUPTHINK, AND LEADERSHIP DYNAMICS

The Iraq War remains one of the most controversial military engagements of the 21st century. The Chilcot Inquiry, published in 2016, sought to examine the decision-making processes involved and to provide an exhaustive account of the United Kingdom's involvement in the conflict. However, beyond its analysis of intelligence failures and military strategies, the Chilcot Report also highlighted critical lessons about leadership authority, the pervasive effects of groupthink, and consequently the absence of psychological safety within the Blair administration. This case study explores these themes through the lens of Irving Janis's groupthink model and examines how the "Dark Triad" of leadership traits—Narcissism, Machiavellianism, and Psychopathy—may have exacerbated these dynamics.

BACKGROUND: THE CONTEXT OF THE IRAQ WAR

In the wake of the 9/11 terrorist attacks, the US-led War on Terror created a global narrative of imminent threats from rogue states. Iraq, under Saddam Hussein's regime, was framed as a critical danger due to allegations of weapons of mass destruction (WMDs). The UK Government under Tony Blair aligned itself with the United States in advocating for military intervention. Blair presented the case for war as a moral imperative, emphasizing Saddam's purported threat to global security.

The Chilcot Inquiry revealed that the decision to go to war was based on flawed intelligence, inadequate debate, and insufficient planning for the post-conflict aftermath. These failings were not merely technical errors but reflected deeper cultural and leadership shortcomings, including a lack of psychological safety and the dominance of Blair's leadership style.

GROUPTHINK AND THE DECISION-MAKING PROCESS

The Chilcot Inquiry provides a textbook example of Janis's groupthink symptoms, which emerge when cohesive groups prioritize consensus over critical thinking. These symptoms explain many of the decision-making failures in the run-up to the Iraq War.

1. Illusion of Invulnerability

The Blair Government exhibited a pervasive overconfidence in its ability to make sound decisions. As one Cabinet member remarked:

> Tony Blair had, as Leader of the Opposition, rescued his party from a very dire political predicament … I had the sense from [Foreign Secretary] Mr Straw's reaction that he had achieved a personal and political dominance.[3]

Blair's previous successes created an aura of invincibility around his leadership, discouraging challenges to his authority. This overconfidence blinded the Cabinet to the risks associated with the decision to invade Iraq and fostered a belief that their actions would inevitably succeed.

2. Rationalization

Warnings and contrary evidence were systematically discounted. For example: despite Tony Blair insisting that Saddam could obtain nuclear weapons within months Chilcot's response was: "That was not so at the time."[4]

Even with the lack of credible intelligence supporting Saddam's imminent nuclear capability, Blair's administration rationalized the need for urgent intervention, framing these unsupported assertions as credible to justify military action.

3. Belief in Inherent Morality

Blair's moral framing of the war further exacerbated groupthink. He argued on several occasions that disarming Saddam was not only necessary but morally right; for example: "I knew in the final analysis I would be with the US, because it was right morally and strategically."[5] This belief in the inherent morality of the mission led to a disregard for ethical concerns, such as the lack of UN authorization for the war and the potential humanitarian consequences of the invasion.

4. Stereotyping of Out-Groups

Saddam Hussein and his regime were demonized to justify military action, particularly the claim that he would provide weapons of mass destruction to terrorist groups, despite the analysis carried out by British intelligence organizations stating that he "was not likely to do so," and that later "There was no credible evidence of covert transfers of WMD-related technology and expertise to terrorist groups."[6]

5. Pressure on Dissenters

Cabinet members who expressed doubts were sidelined. Chilcot noted:

> We asked how it was that members of the Cabinet—other than [former Foreign Secretary] Robin Cook and, to a lesser extent, [Secretary of State for International Development] Clare Short—did not provide more challenge and insist on

debate and information. They were promised it sometimes, but the promises were not delivered.[7]

The lack of follow-through on promises of debate discouraged dissent, effectively forcing conformity within the Cabinet. Robin Cook, a Cabinet member who wasn't against a military invasion, made it clear that the intelligence reports could be read in different ways. Rather than being listened to and his perspective debated, Chilcot says that his thoughts were met with "passivity."[8]

6. Self-Censorship

Many Cabinet members suppressed their own doubts, assuming Blair's judgment was infallible. "It was about the dominance and authority Mr. Blair had acquired by his political success in '97 and again in '01. That didn't mean that they were pusillanimous, necessarily, but I think they had a faith in his being right, and it was not for them to say, 'No, Tony, you're wrong.'" Blair's standing, authority, and dominance led to self-censorship among his colleagues, who hesitated to voice their concerns, fearing they might undermine the collective narrative.

7. Illusion of Unanimity

The lack of substantive Cabinet discussions created a false sense of consensus:

There was no collective discussion of the decision by senior Ministers.[9]

By avoiding open debate, the Blair administration perpetuated the illusion that the decision to go to war was unanimous, even though private doubts persisted among members.

8. Mindguards

There were not mindguards in the way Janis described the concept, and in some respects, it was the prime minister himself who was the mindguard, presenting information to the Cabinet and the public more generally, which emphasized certain aspects that supported his point of view, to the neglect of others. Key information and dissenting views were shielded from the broader Cabinet:

> The Prime Minister said, "I will have the official committee … but not a ministerial committee."

Blair's decision to bypass broader ministerial discussions, via a ministerial committee, ensured that critical perspectives were excluded from the decision-making process.

9. Direct Pressure on Dissenters

The report makes clear that the information was not presented in an objective and unbiased way in order to solicit debate. "Intelligence and assessments were used to prepare material to be used to support Government statements in a way which conveyed certainty without acknowledging the limitations of the intelligence."[10] The key dissenter, Robin Cook, eventually resigned from the Cabinet because of the lack of willingness to consider alternative points of view. The Chilcot report acknowledges that the absence of a critical voice like Cook's meant that discussions lacked sufficient challenge.

LEADERSHIP STYLE

Blair's leadership style further entrenched groupthink. His dominance and authority over the party were a result of his returning the Labour Party to power.

> Tony Blair had, as Leader of the Opposition, rescued his party from a very dire political predicament and he had done that

again afterwards as Prime Minister ... he had achieved a personal and political dominance that was itself overriding, if you like, the doctrine of collective Cabinet responsibility.

In his oral evidence, Chilcot agreed that the power of privilege and patronage holds back discussion, but in addition to that, it was "also, just sheer political dominance. He had been right; was he not right this time?"

Blair's overconfidence in his moral vision and his belief in his ability to influence US policy discouraged dissent and created a culture of deference.

Blair's control over information flow and strategic use of patronage to suppress opposition demonstrate an ultimately self-serving approach to maintaining power.

While Blair did not exhibit overtly psychopathic traits, his willingness to bypass collective decision-making processes and minimize ethical concerns aligns with elements of psychopathic leadership.

CONCLUSION

The Chilcot Inquiry highlights how groupthink, exacerbated by leadership dominance and the absence of psychological safety, can lead to catastrophic decision-making failures. Tony Blair's leadership style, marked by overconfidence, moral certainty, and control over dissent, created an environment where critical thinking was suppressed, and flawed decisions went unchallenged. The Iraq War serves as a cautionary tale of the dangers of groupthink and the importance of fostering psychological safety in leadership and decision-making processes. By examining these failures, future leaders can learn to prioritize transparency, encourage dissent, and create environments where critical voices are not only tolerated but valued.

CASE STUDY: EMPATHY, LEADERSHIP, AND SUCCESS—THE SATYA NADELLA STORY

When Satya Nadella became CEO of Microsoft in February 2014, he faced an uphill battle. The tech giant, once synonymous with innovation, had become a symbol of stagnation. Bureaucracy stifled creativity, internal politics replaced teamwork, and the company was rapidly falling behind its competitors. As Nadella observed, "Innovation was being replaced by bureaucracy. Teamwork was being replaced by internal politics. We were falling behind."[11] Microsoft was in dire need of not just a new strategy, but a new soul.

In stark contrast to the leadership failures chronicled in the previous case study, where groupthink and dominance led to very poor decision-making, Nadella's journey at Microsoft exemplifies how empathy, humility, and collaboration can transform not only a company but its people. This case study shows how Nadella hit "refresh" on Microsoft, proving that empathetic leadership is not just compatible with business success—it's essential for it.

STEPPING INTO LEADERSHIP: A FRESH PERSPECTIVE

In his memoir *Hit Refresh*, Nadella reflects on the qualities Bill Gates, Microsoft's founder, appreciated and encouraged in leaders, namely individuals who were innovative, pragmatic, and forward-looking. Gates himself is quoted as saying that Nadella raised "smart questions about our strategy," reflecting Nadella's ability to think critically and provide fresh perspectives.[12]

When Nadella was considered for the CEO role, Gates reportedly supported his candidacy because of his ability to combine technical expertise with a deep understanding of business strategy. Gates also saw Nadella's collaborative and empathetic leadership style as a crucial quality for guiding Microsoft into a new era. Nadella recalls that Gates remained involved even after his appointment, agreeing to serve as his advisor on product innovation during the transition.

On being appointed as Microsoft's third CEO, he made it clear from the outset that his focus would be on culture. "Renewing our company's culture would be my highest priority," he told employees.[13] Nadella believed deeply that a company's success depended not just on its products but on its people. "We spend far too much time at work for it not to have deep meaning," he said. "My personal philosophy … is to connect new ideas with a growing sense of empathy for other people. Ideas excite me. Empathy grounds and centers me."[14]

One of his first acts as CEO was to bring his senior leadership team together for a retreat—not to discuss strategy or finances, but to reflect on themselves. Nadella asked his team to share their personal philosophies, passions, and even fears. This wasn't easy. As Nadella later reflected, "The answers were hard to pull out … Fear: of being ridiculed; of failing; of not looking like the smartest person in the room. And arrogance: I am too important for these games."[15]

What emerged from these sessions was a sense of shared humanity. Leaders dropped their defenses and connected on a deeper level. Nadella believed this was critical: "We needed to deepen our understanding of one another … and to connect our personal philosophies to our jobs as leaders."[16] It was a small but significant step in breaking down the barriers of mistrust and fostering a culture of psychological safety.

LEADING WITH EMPATHY

Empathy became the cornerstone of Nadella's leadership. It is clear that this is more than a quality to be developed, and it certainly wasn't just a buzzword; it was a guiding principle. Reflecting on his life experiences, Nadella shared how empathy had shaped him, particularly as the father of a son with severe disabilities.

I have empathy for people with disabilities. I have empathy for small business owners working to succeed. I have empathy for any person targeted with violence and hate because of the color of his or her skin, what they believe, or who they love.[17]

Critically, empathy wasn't just a moral stance—it was a driver of innovation. Under Nadella's leadership, Microsoft developed eye-gaze tracking technology to help individuals with ALS (Amyotrophic Lateral Sclerosis-a progressive condition that damages motor neurons, causing muscle weakness and paralysis) and cerebral palsy gain independence. This wasn't just a product innovation; it was a powerful example of how deeply understanding others' needs could inspire solutions that changed lives.

EMBRACING HUMILITY AND VULNERABILITY

Nadella wasn't afraid to show vulnerability, even when it meant admitting mistakes. One of the most public examples came early in his tenure when he mishandled a question about gender bias at a women's tech conference. Asked what advice he had for women seeking pay raises, Nadella suggested they trust the system to reward them over time—a response that was immediately criticized. Reflecting on the incident, and in a remarkable confession, Nadella wrote, "I'm glad I messed up in such a public forum because it helped me confront an unconscious bias I didn't know I had."[18]

Rather than deflect blame or double down, Nadella sent an email to all employees acknowledging his mistake and committing to learn from it. "Leaders need to act and shape the culture to root out biases," he wrote. This moment of humility struck a chord with employees, reinforcing Nadella's commitment to fostering an inclusive and equitable culture—something that helps to build trust.

TRANSFORMING MICROSOFT: A CULTURE OF TRUST AND COLLABORATION

Microsoft's internal culture had long been characterized by silos and competition among teams. Nadella recognized that this "winner-takes-all" mentality was holding the company back. To address this, he emphasized the importance of collaboration, even with external rivals. "Partnering is too often seen as a zero-sum game," he said. "When done right, partnering grows the pie for everyone."[19]

This philosophy extended to competitors like Apple and Amazon. Despite initial resistance from within Microsoft, Nadella pursued partnerships that prioritized customer needs over company rivalries. For example, Microsoft worked with Apple to optimize Office 365 for the iPad Pro, and Bing powered search on Amazon Fire tablets. These collaborations not only expanded Microsoft's reach but also demonstrated the power of putting customers first.

Nadella's approach to leadership also meant empowering his teams to take ownership of their work. He met individually with leaders to build consensus around a "cloud-first" strategy, even when it required moving away from Microsoft's traditional server-based software. By listening, empathizing, and building trust, Nadella turned skeptics into believers and successfully transitioned Microsoft to a cloud-first model.

THE RESULTS: A REVITALIZED MICROSOFT

The impact of Nadella's leadership was profound. Within three years, Microsoft's market value tripled, and the company regained its reputation as a leader in innovation. Employees reported feeling more optimistic and engaged.

Nadella's leadership also made Microsoft a more inclusive and empathetic organization. His efforts to address unconscious bias and create opportunities for underrepresented groups sent a powerful message: success and empathy are not mutually exclusive.

As Nadella observed, "Anyone who feels like an outsider can be successful, but it requires both an enlightened management and a dedicated employee."[20]

A POSITIVE CASE STUDY IN LEADERSHIP

Nadella's story is a powerful counter-narrative to the belief that leadership must be authoritative or cutthroat to succeed. His emphasis on empathy, humility, and collaboration revitalized Microsoft, proving that compassionate leadership can drive both cultural and financial success.

This case study stands in stark contrast to the previous example of groupthink and authoritarian leadership, where dissent was silenced and ethical considerations were sidelined. Nadella's approach demonstrates the value of fostering psychological safety, encouraging open dialogue, and leading with empathy.

For leaders who may doubt the effectiveness of these qualities, Nadella's transformation of Microsoft offers a clear message: being empathetic and supportive doesn't just feel good—it works. As Nadella himself put it, "Empathy is a crucial ingredient … It grounds and centers me."[21] By grounding leadership in empathy and humility, Nadella not only turned Microsoft around but also set a new standard for what leadership can achieve.

KEY POINTS

Authority, by itself, is not inherently good or bad—it is a neutral force shaped by how it is wielded. In Stanley Milgram's famous experiments, authority figures used their position to prompt participants into harmful actions. This misuse of power illustrates the darker side of authority, where individuals relinquish personal responsibility under its weight. Yet, authority can also be a force for good, guiding teams toward shared goals and ethical outcomes.

The challenge for leaders is finding the balance: how to provide the structure and direction needed for success while respecting the autonomy and humanity of their team members. Recognizing the psychological pressures authority places on individuals is a critical step in using it responsibly.

Authority, groupthink, and leadership personality are all interconnected forces shaping organizational culture. As the case studies demonstrate, leaders hold immense power to either cultivate trust and collaboration or perpetuate submissiveness and dysfunction. The path to success lies in striking a balance: addressing the toxic traits of the Dark Triad while actively fostering the inclusive qualities of the Light Triad.

By embedding psychological safety into the fabric of their organizations, leaders can ensure that their authority is wielded responsibly, decisions are made thoughtfully, and teams are empowered to reach their full potential. The ultimate takeaway? Empathy and ethical leadership are not just compatible with success—they are essential to achieving it. In embracing these principles, leaders can create workplaces where individuals and teams truly flourish.

Have the lessons been learned? I suppose the best answer I can try to give to that is that we cannot know yet, because the real test will be the take-up of the lessons that we sought to draw and others may indeed find. That is going to be a process, looking ahead, that will take some time. As things stand at present, it is notable the decisions that led to the Iraq war have been subject to public scrutiny. However, the typical response of governments is to appoint lawyers to conduct such inquiries. The recommendations tend to focus on process, governance, and structure, with little consideration given to the psychological and environmental factors. Issues like groupthink and psychological safety, therefore, are given insufficient consideration, thereby increasing the likelihood that such mistakes will be repeated.

GLOSSARY

Obedience to authority. The act of following instructions or orders from someone perceived as an authority figure, even if they clash with personal beliefs or values. Stanley Milgram's classic experiments showed how social and situational factors influenced individuals to comply with authority, sometimes doing things that they would not normally do. He also revealed the factors that were present when people did not obey, which help to reinforce the importance of psychological safety.

Groupthink. A situation where the desire for harmony or agreement in a group leads to poor decision-making. It happens when group members prioritize consensus over critical thinking, reality testing, and ethical judgment. This can result not only in flawed choices but the suppression of dissenting opinions.

The Dark Triad. A group of three personality traits—Machiavellianism, Narcissism, and Psychopathy—that are associated with manipulative and harmful behaviors:

- **Machiavellianism**: Strategic manipulation, deception, and exploitation of others for personal gain, often at the expense of ethics and relationships.
- **Narcissism**: Excessive self-admiration, entitlement, and a lack of empathy, often leading to a focus on self-image over collaboration.
- **Psychopathy**: Impulsivity, emotional coldness, and a lack of remorse, resulting in exploitative and reckless behavior.

These traits have a significant impact on psychological safety.

The Light Triad. A set of personality traits—empathy, compassion, and cooperation—that promote meaningful relationships and psychological safety. These traits act as a counterbalance to the harm caused by manipulative behaviors, fostering trust, collaboration, and innovation.

The Light Triad is linked to **Organizational Citizenship Behaviors** (OCBs)—voluntary actions like mentoring, conflict resolution, and boosting team morale. These behaviors strengthen workplace culture, improve productivity, and build cohesive teams.

NOTES

1 Janis, I.L. (1982). *Groupthink.* 2nd ed. Houghton Mifflin, p. 9.
2 Janis, I.L. (1982). *Groupthink.* 2nd ed. Houghton Mifflin, p. 42.
3 UK Parliament (2016). *Oral evidence: Follow up to the Chilcot Report. HC 689*, House of Commons Liaison Committee, 2 November. Available at: https://committees.parliament.uk/oralevidence/588/html/ [Accessed 10 July 2025].
4 UK Parliament (2016). *Oral evidence: Follow up to the Chilcot Report. HC 689*, House of Commons Liaison Committee, 2 November. Available at: https://committees.parliament.uk/oralevidence/588/html/ [Accessed 10 July 2025].
5 Chilcot, J. (2016). *The report of the Iraq inquiry: Executive summary.* London: The Stationery Office. Available at: https://webarchive .nationalarchives.gov.uk/ukgwa/20171123123237/http://www .iraqinquiry.org.uk/media/246416/the-report-of-the-iraq-inquiry _executive-summary.pdf [Accessed 10 July 2025].
6 Chilcot, J. (2016). The report of the Iraq inquiry: Executive summary, p. 43.
7 House of Commons Liaison Committee Oral evidence: Follow-up to the Chilcot report, HC689, 2 November 2016.
8 House of Commons Liaison Committee Oral evidence: Follow-up to the Chilcot report, HC689, 2 November 2016.
9 Chilcot, J. (2016). The report of the Iraq inquiry: Executive summary, p. 22. .
10 Chilcot, J. (2016). The report of the Iraq inquiry: Executive summary, p. 46.
11 Nadella S. (2017). *Hit Refresh: The Quest to Rediscover Microsoft's Soul and Imagine a Better Future for Everyone.* HarperCollins, p. 11.
12 Nadella, S., 2017. *Hit refresh: The quest to rediscover Microsoft's Soul and imagine a better future for everyone.* Harper Collins, p. 8.

13 Nadella, S., 2017. *Hit refresh: The quest to rediscover Microsoft's Soul and imagine a better future for everyone*. Harper Collins, p. 12.

14 Nadella, S., 2017. *Hit refresh: The quest to rediscover Microsoft's Soul and imagine a better future for everyone*. Harper Collins, pp. 16–17.

15 Nadella, S., 2017. *Hit refresh: The quest to rediscover Microsoft's Soul and imagine a better future for everyone*. Harper Collins, p. 14.

16 Nadella, S., 2017. *Hit refresh: The quest to rediscover Microsoft's Soul and imagine a better future for everyone*. Harper Collins, p. 13.

17 Nadella, S., 2017. *Hit refresh: The quest to rediscover Microsoft's Soul and imagine a better future for everyone*. Harper Collins, p. 18.

18 Nadella, S., 2017. *Hit refresh: The quest to rediscover Microsoft's Soul and imagine a better future for everyone*. Harper Collins, p. 108.

19 Nadella, S., 2017. *Hit refresh: The quest to rediscover Microsoft's Soul and imagine a better future for everyone*. Harper Collins, p. 116.

20 Nadella, S., 2017. *Hit refresh: The quest to rediscover Microsoft's Soul and imagine a better future for everyone*. Harper Collins, p. 111.

21 Nadella, S., 2017. *Hit refresh: The quest to rediscover Microsoft's Soul and imagine a better future for everyone*. Harper Collins, p. 16

FURTHER READING

Janis, I.L., 1982. *Groupthink*. 2nd ed. Houghton Mifflin.

LeBreton, J.M., Shiverdecker, L.K. and Grimaldi, E.M., 2018. The dark triad and workplace behavior. *Annual Review of Organizational Psychology and Organizational Behavior*, 5(1), pp. 387–414.

Milgram, S., 1974. *Obedience to authority: An experimental view*. Harper and Row.

Nadella, S., 2017. *Hit refresh: The quest to rediscover Microsoft's Soul and imagine a better future for everyone*. Harper Collins.

Schein, Edgar H. and Schein, Peter A., 2017. *Humble leadership: The power of relationships, openness, and trust*. Berrett-Koehler Publishers.

6

WHAT IF I'M THE ONLY DISSENTER IN A TEAM?

INTRODUCTION

Imagine this: you're sitting in a brightly lit room with six other people, all of you about to take part in what seems like a straightforward psychology experiment. The atmosphere is casual and people are chatting softly, curious about what's to come. Then the group is shown two large cards. On one card, there's a single vertical black line—the "standard" line. On the other card are three vertical lines of different lengths. The task is simple enough: figure out which of the three lines matches the length of the standard.

You are the last one in line, so you hear everyone else's responses. One by one, the answers come, and everyone agrees on the correct line. The process is repetitive but straightforward.

But then, something weird happens. After a couple of rounds, the group unanimously gives an answer that is *clearly wrong*. You look more intently at the lines again—there's no doubt about it. The correct answer is obvious. Yet everyone is confidently agreeing on the same wrong choice.

As always, you are the last to give your response; your turn is coming, and now you're starting to feel uneasy. You glance at the faces around you. They seem calm, unfazed, completely at ease with their blatantly wrong answer. And then the doubt creeps in.

DOI: 10.4324/9781003501855-8

Did I miss something? Is there some trick I'm not seeing? Or—what if *I'm* the one who's wrong?

The moment arrives, and all eyes are on you. You sense your heartbeat quicken; you feel tense. You know what you see, but do you stick with your own judgment, or do you go along with the group? It's such a simple task—just comparing the lengths of lines—but in that moment, it feels like so much more. What do you do?

This was the setup of Solomon Asch's famous experiments on conformity conducted in the 1950s.[1] The goal was to explore how social pressure influences individual judgment. The results were striking and have profound implications for understanding human behavior and the environments we create—especially when it comes to fostering what we now call psychological safety.

THE POWER OF SOCIAL PRESSURE

In Asch's study, 123 participants were placed in this minority position across multiple trials. They faced two opposing forces: the unambiguous evidence of their eyes versus the unanimous opinion of the group. The results were indeed eye-opening. When faced with group pressure, a significant number of participants—36.8%—yielded at least once, agreeing with the majority's incorrect answers. This is notable because, left to their own devices without group influence, participants made errors less than 1% of the time. The mere presence of a unanimous majority increased conformity dramatically.

(Earlier studies from the 1930s by the psychologist was Muzafer Sherif, who obtained similar results, posed the questions: What is truth and how is it formed?[2])

It is important to note that not everyone conformed. Around 25% of participants remained firmly independent, consistently choosing the correct answer despite the group's pressure. At the other extreme, some individuals conformed nearly every time the group gave an incorrect answer. These results revealed a range of responses to social pressure, from complete independence to full compliance.

WHY DO PEOPLE CONFORM?

Asch's interviews with participants shed light on their reasoning. Those who conformed often did so because they:

- doubted their own perceptions, assuming, "I must be wrong; they can't all be mistaken."
- wanted to avoid conflict, placing group harmony over their own judgment.
- feared that dissenting would make them appear foolish or difficult, so they chose to blend in with the group.

On the other hand, those who resisted group pressure:

- often expressed strong confidence in their own judgment.
- felt it was their duty to state the truth as they saw it, regardless of what others said.

It is important to note that this group wasn't immune to self-doubt; they simply found ways to recover from it and reaffirm their independence.

THE ROLE OF UNANIMITY AND DISSENT

Asch explored additional factors that influenced conformity, such as the size and unanimity of the majority. It only took a majority of three people to create significant pressure; adding more individuals had little additional effect.

One of the most powerful findings, however, came from introducing a single dissenting voice into the group. When even one other person gave the correct answer, conformity rates dropped dramatically. This effect occurred even if the dissenting individual was incorrect but still broke the group's unanimity. The mere presence of a dissenter emboldened participants to trust their own judgment. It provided emotional reassurance that disagreement was possible and a sense of solidarity, even if the dissenter's opinion didn't agree with their own.

The conformity effect has been found in replications of the study in other parts of the world,[3] including more recently Bosnia Herzegovina[4] (where 35.4% conformed to the majority). Studies in Japan have also confirmed the effect there,[5] with one showing, contrary to belief, that Japanese participants, coming from a collectivist society, were no more conforming than the individualistic Americans.[6]

Social influence extends far beyond simple tasks like judging the length of lines—it deeply affects people's attitudes and decisions, even on significant issues like political opinions. Building on Asch's original research, a recent Swiss study[7] demonstrates that the power of group pressure can shape political attitudes in striking ways. Rather than being faced with people misdiagnosing the length of a line, participants were exposed to group opinions concerning five different political statements. Researchers observed an average conformity rate of 38%, echoing Asch's findings and confirming the broader applicability of social influence. For example, when the group expressed support for giving the Swiss Federal Council more power, 27% of participants aligned with the group's opinion. In contrast, when the group opposed the idea, only 3% agreed with giving the council more power, a dramatic 23.4% difference.

Similarly, the study found that giving support for trade unions increased to 72% when the group favored it, compared to only 29% when the group opposed it—a whopping difference of 43%. The same pattern was seen in questions about employers' associations, citizens' liberties, and corporate freedom. Across all five questions, group pressure consistently swayed participants, demonstrating that we are highly influenced by the majority's stance even when conformity is not limited to simple perceptual tasks but extends to attitudes and beliefs. The findings also suggest that susceptibility to group influence transcends intelligence, self-esteem, or the Big Five personality dimensions, with the exception of openness. The researchers even found conformity when people were financially incentivized to express their own opinion.

WHAT DOES THIS TELL US ABOUT PSYCHOLOGICAL SAFETY AND INDEPENDENCE?

Asch's experiments highlight how the fear of standing out or being judged can suppress our willingness to express our true thoughts. Even when the evidence is clear, the weight of social pressure can lead individuals to conform, choosing group consensus over independent judgment.

Asch's findings show the importance of creating spaces where dissent is not only tolerated but actively encouraged. Significantly, the presence of even one dissenting voice can disrupt conformity and foster a culture of open dialogue and critical thinking.

THE HIDDEN COSTS OF CONFORMITY

Asch's work also warns of the dangers of unchecked conformity. When individuals suppress their true thoughts to align with everyone else, the entire group's decision-making process suffers. Errors go unchallenged, critical insights are lost, and the potential for innovation diminishes.

For example, take a typical corporate meeting, where a team is deciding on an important strategy, and most people, including senior leaders, are strongly in favor of one idea. One team member has concerns about the plan and thinks there might be a better option. However, seeing everyone else so confident and not wanting to cause conflict or seem out of place, they don't just stay quiet but agree with the others. The decision goes ahead as planned, but later it becomes clear that the chosen strategy was flawed and a better option was overlooked. This example shows how group pressure and a lack of open communication can lead to poor decisions, especially when people feel they can't speak up about their concerns.

WHAT ARE THE LESSONS FOR ORGANIZATIONS?

Asch's experiments provide a blueprint for fostering psychological safety in teams and organizations. Here are key takeaways:

1. **Encourage Dissent**: Just as a single dissenting voice reduced conformity in Asch's studies, organizations should create cultures where diverse opinions are welcomed. Leaders can set the tone by actively inviting alternative perspectives and rewarding critical thinking.
2. **Reduce Fear of Reprisal**: Fear of standing out or being wrong often drives conformity. Leaders must ensure that individuals feel safe to express their views without fear of negative consequences. This might include setting clear guidelines for respectful communication and reinforcing that disagreements are a natural part of collaboration.
3. **Celebrate Independence**: Organizations should recognize and celebrate individuals who display independent thinking. Highlighting these behaviors reinforces their value and encourages others to follow suit.
4. **Train Leaders to Listen**: In Asch's studies, dissenting voices were often ignored or dismissed. Leaders must be trained to listen actively and thoughtfully to all contributions, especially those that challenge the status quo.
5. **Break Unanimity**: In decision-making processes, unanimity can be a red flag. Encourage individuals to look at the issue from different perspectives to surface potential blind spots and avoid groupthink.

While Asch's findings reveal the strong pull of conformity, they also highlight the resilience of independence. Many participants resisted group pressure, trusting their own perceptions or feeling a responsibility to speak the truth. This demonstrates that, even in the face of overwhelming social pressure, people still have the capacity to stand firm. For organizations, this is a reminder that psychological safety doesn't just protect individuals from harm; it unlocks their potential to contribute meaningfully and authentically.

Asch's experiments remain a powerful illustration of how social dynamics shape behavior. They remind us that creating psychologically safe environments isn't just about reducing fear; it's about empowering individuals to think critically, speak openly, and challenge the status quo. In doing so, organizations can foster not only better decision-making but also greater innovation and resilience.

PSYCHOLOGICAL SAFETY IN TEAMS: LESSONS FROM GOOGLE'S PROJECT ARISTOTLE[8]

Launched in 2012, Project Aristotle sought to answer a deceptively simple question: What makes a team effective? Google's People Operations department, renowned for its data-driven approach to human resource management, analyzed over 180 teams across the company. The initiative was inspired by Aristotle's assertion that "the whole is greater than the sum of its parts," reflecting a belief that team success involves more than just individual excellence.

At the outset, Google hypothesized that team effectiveness was rooted in assembling the "right" people—those with the highest skills, expertise, and individual performance metrics. To their surprise, the brilliance of individual team members had little correlation with team success. Instead, the project revealed a more profound truth about teamwork: it's not who is on the team that matters, but how the team works together.

SHIFTING THE FOCUS: GROUP NORMS OVER INDIVIDUAL TALENT

As the research progressed, the focus shifted from individual capabilities to a far more significant predictor of team performance: group norms. These are unwritten rules that govern team behavior and influence how teams communicate, handle disagreements, and collaborate. Teams composed of high-performing individuals often struggled if their norms did not promote effective collaboration. In other words, group norms could override individual brilliance. Conversely, teams with less individually impressive members often excelled when their norms encouraged open communication, mutual respect, and shared responsibility. Results showing this type of effect have indicated that this is a factor in swimming relay teams.

The most important revelation from Project Aristotle was the critical role of psychological safety. Teams with high psychological safety fostered an environment where members felt free to be themselves. They could admit mistakes, ask questions, and share ideas without fear of ridicule. This openness not only reduced stress but also unlocked creativity and innovation.

In addition to psychological safety, two other norms emerged as vital to team performance:

1. **Equality in Conversation Turn-Taking**: High-performing teams ensured that all members had an equal opportunity to speak. The sense of inclusion made every team member feel valued and engaged.
2. **High Social Sensitivity**: Successful teams were composed of individuals who were attuned to each other's emotions and needs. This emotional intelligence allowed team members to pick up on subtle cues, such as when someone was feeling excluded or overwhelmed, and adjust their behavior accordingly.

Conventional wisdom suggested that teams working in close physical proximity or composed of similar personalities would perform better. Yet, Google's data revealed no significant correlation between these factors and team success. Geographically dispersed teams could perform just as well as co-located ones if they cultivated the right norms. Similarly, diversity in backgrounds and personalities posed no barrier to success when psychological safety was present.

As we saw in Chapter 3, the findings from Project Aristotle extend far beyond the tech world. Whether in healthcare, education, sports, or hospitality, the principles of psychological safety and collaborative norms are universally applicable. For example, a hospital team might focus on creating a safe space for discussing medical errors without fear of blame, while a sports team might prioritize camaraderie and mutual trust.[9]

Importantly, the research also challenges traditional talent management strategies. It shifts the focus from hiring superstar individuals to building cohesive, supportive teams. It also highlights the limitations of metrics like individual output or technical skills in predicting team success. Instead, organizations should evaluate team dynamics, psychological safety, and emotional intelligence as key indicators of performance.

In the end, the most important ingredient in any team is not just talent but trust, empathy, and connection.

THE WORK OF AMY EDMONDSON

While Google's findings gave the idea of psychological safety in teams a major push forward, they didn't occur in a vacuum. As was mentioned in Chapter 2, a key figure in the field of psychological safety is Professor Amy Edmondson, who has written best-selling books, including *The Fearless Organization* and *Teaming*, sharing the results of her work and her insights.

The Fearless Organization explores the importance of creating a climate of psychological safety primarily in stable teams, where individuals feel safe to speak up, admit mistakes, and contribute their ideas without fear of embarrassment or punishment. *Teaming* builds on this foundation by addressing the unique challenges of modern, fluid, and cross-functional collaborations, where teams are often temporary and assembled to address specific, complex problems.

Based on her two books, *The Fearless Organization* and *Teaming*, we can identify ten key features of a psychologically safe team:

1. Cultivate an Open and Inclusive Leadership Style

   - **Be Approachable**: Schedule regular one-on-one check-ins where team members can share ideas or concerns without judgment.
   - **Admit Vulnerability**: Share a time you made a mistake and what you learned from it. This sets the tone for openness.
   - **Actively Listen**: When team members speak, focus fully on them—acknowledge their input with thoughtful responses or follow-up actions.

2. Frame the Work with Shared Purpose and Clarity

   - **Define the "Why"**: Start meetings or project kick-offs by explicitly stating why the work matters and its broader impact.
   - **Use Visual Tools**: Create a shared dashboard or goal board that links individual contributions to team and organizational objectives.
   - **Revisit Purpose**: Regularly reinforce how tasks align with the team's mission to keep focus and motivation high.

3. Normalize Mistakes as Learning Opportunities

   - **Reframe Failure**: Use language like "What did we learn?" instead of "What went wrong?" in post-project reviews.
   - **Set an Example**: Acknowledge your own mistakes publicly and share how they shaped your thinking.
   - **Celebrate Learning**: Recognize team members for the risks they take and the lessons they bring back, even when outcomes aren't perfect.

4. Actively Invite and Encourage Participation

- **Rotate Facilitation**: Have different team members lead meetings to give everyone a voice.
- **Create Structures for Input**: Use tools like anonymous polls, suggestion boards, or pre-meeting surveys to ensure all ideas are heard.
- **Watch for Patterns**: Observe who tends to dominate discussions and gently redirect the conversation to quieter members.

5. Respond Productively to Input

- **Acknowledge Ideas**: Thank team members for their input, even if it's not immediately actionable.
- **Ask Clarifying Questions**: Show interest by asking follow-up questions that demonstrate you value their perspective.
- **Provide Feedback**: If an idea isn't feasible, explain why respectfully and discuss alternative solutions together.

6. Encourage Experimentation and Risk-Taking

- **Reward Effort, Not Just Results**: Acknowledge the courage it takes to try something new, even if it doesn't work out.
- **Create Safe Zones**: Dedicate a part of your team's process to testing and experimentation where outcomes are treated as learning opportunities.
- **Set Expectations**: Communicate that innovation often involves setbacks and highlight stories where calculated risks led to breakthroughs.

7. Foster Collaboration and Mutual Respect

- **Model Collaboration**: As a leader, openly collaborate with your team and show respect for their expertise.
- **Encourage Peer Feedback**: Create a culture where team members routinely recognize and appreciate each other's work.

- **Celebrate Group Achievements**: Highlight not just individual contributions but how collaboration led to success.

8. Break Down Barriers to Speaking Up

- **Address Hierarchy**: Actively involve junior team members or quieter voices in discussions by asking for their input.
- **Reward Dissent**: Show appreciation when team members respectfully challenge decisions or provide alternative viewpoints.
- **Conduct Anonymous Reviews**: Allow team members to voice concerns anonymously to uncover unspoken barriers.

9. Build Reflection into Team Processes

- **Implement retrospectives**: After each project or milestone, hold a structured discussion to reflect on what worked and what didn't.
- **Use Reflection Tools**: Incorporate exercises like Start/Stop/Continue or SWOT analyses to evaluate team dynamics.
- **Share Insights**: Document and circulate key lessons from reflections so the team can track progress over time.

10. Establish Clear Boundaries and Accountability

- **Define Roles Upfront**: Clearly outline responsibilities at the start of each project or initiative to minimize confusion.
- **Set Behavioral Norms**: Collaboratively agree on ground rules for interactions, such as respecting speaking turns or timelines.
- **Follow through on Accountability**: Hold team members to their commitments in a fair and transparent way, reinforcing trust and dependability.

These actions aren't just theoretical—they're observable, repeatable, and adaptable for any organization aiming to build high-performing, psychologically safe teams.

PSYCHOLOGICAL SAFETY IN VIRTUAL TEAMS: APPLYING EDMONDSON'S TEN PRINCIPLES

Virtual team working is something that is a recognized part of working life, and this was accelerated during the pandemic. Google's Project Aristotle stated that, as long as there was psychological safety, virtual and all-remote team working was just as effective as those meeting and working face-to-face.

As social beings, we naturally gravitate toward those with whom we share similarities, for example, language, cultural background, or even proximity, such as sitting in the same office. This tendency to classify ourselves into groups based on perceived commonalities creates in-groups within teams. These in-groups often foster strong bonds and trust among their members, but at the same time, they can inadvertently exclude those who fall outside their circle (this will be explored in more depth in Chapter 8). In face-to-face environments, spontaneous and informal interactions—encounters by the water cooler, impromptu chats in the hallway, or shared moments leaving a meeting room—provide opportunities for diverse team members to connect. These casual interactions can help to dilute the exclusivity of in-groups, enhancing team-wide inclusivity and shared understanding.[10]

In virtual teams, however, there is a dramatic shift. Online interactions are more formal, structured, and deliberate, with little room for spontaneity. Team members often form "bubbles," selectively interacting with a small, familiar group of colleagues while inadvertently excluding others. These bubbles reinforce in-group bonds but create barriers for those outside the circle, who may find it increasingly difficult to reach out or feel included. The result is less team inclusion where psychological safety suffers—knowledge sharing becomes constrained, trust erodes, and team performance declines.

Remote working also demands greater autonomy and self-leadership on the part of every team member.[11] The increased formality of virtual working makes it more difficult for people to reach out for help from their colleagues.[12]

Research evidence provides us with guidance on how to manage virtual teams in order to create psychological safety.[13] [14]

The good news, though, is that we should remind ourselves that Google's Project Aristotle revealed that high-performing teams, whether virtual or face-to-face, share one crucial characteristic: a strong sense of psychological safety. The same principles that promote psychological safety in traditional environments are equally relevant for virtual teams, although the specific actions to address virtual challenges may differ.

By applying the 10 principles to virtual teams, we can build on an established foundation while recognizing the unique circumstances of remote work environments.

THE TEN PRINCIPLES AND THEIR APPLICATION TO VIRTUAL TEAMS

1. Cultivate an Open and Inclusive Leadership Style

   Application to Virtual Teams: Leaders in virtual teams need to be deliberate in creating an approachable and inclusive environment. This involves scheduling regular one-on-one check-ins via video or other communication tools and sharing their own vulnerabilities to encourage openness.

   - Schedule frequent one-on-one virtual check-ins to create space for team members to share concerns.
   - Admit to some personal mistakes during virtual meetings to set a tone of humility and openness.
   - Actively listen and respond to virtual team members with thoughtful follow-ups.

2. Frame the Work with Shared Purpose and Clarity
   Application to Virtual Teams: Virtual teams often lack the natural reinforcement of shared goals that comes from physical proximity. Leaders should emphasize clear objectives and ensure team members understand how their contributions align with broader goals.

   • Begin virtual meetings by articulating the team's purpose and how individual tasks contribute to it.
   • Use shared online dashboards to visualize progress and connections to organizational goals.
   • Periodically revisit team goals to maintain focus and alignment.

3. Normalize Mistakes as Learning Opportunities
   Application to Virtual Teams: Virtual teams may fear making mistakes more due to the lack of informal interactions that build trust. Leaders must intentionally create a culture where failure is seen as part of learning.

   • Reframe post-project reviews as opportunities to discuss lessons learned rather than mistakes made.
   • Model vulnerability by acknowledging personal failures or acknowledgement that they don't have all the answers during team calls.
   • Celebrate team members who take risks and share insights from both successes and setbacks.

4. Actively Invite and Encourage Participation
   Application to Virtual Teams: Virtual environments can make it harder for some voices to be heard.

   • Leaders need to create proactively opportunities for everyone to contribute.
   • Rotate meeting facilitation roles to ensure all team members have a voice. Use anonymous surveys or virtual suggestion tools to gather input.
   • Monitor discussions and invite quieter participants to share their thoughts.

5. Respond Productively to Input
   Application to Virtual Teams: Remote team members may hesitate to share ideas if they feel their input won't be valued. Leaders need to demonstrate active engagement with suggestions.

   - Thank team members for their contributions during virtual meetings.
   - Ask clarifying questions to demonstrate genuine interest in their ideas.
   - Provide respectful feedback and explore alternative solutions collaboratively.

6. Encourage Experimentation and Risk-Taking
   Application to Virtual Teams: The lack of informal camaraderie in virtual teams can discourage risk-taking. Leaders should establish virtual "safe zones" for experimentation.

   - Dedicate parts of virtual meetings to brainstorming or pilot-testing ideas.
   - Celebrate attempts to innovate, even if they do not lead to immediate success.
   - Highlight examples of successful experimentation to encourage others.

7. Foster Collaboration and Mutual Respect
   Application to Virtual Teams: Building interpersonal connections in virtual teams requires intentional effort. Leaders should encourage activities that foster mutual respect and collaboration.

   - Organize virtual team-building activities to strengthen interpersonal bonds.
   - Encourage peer recognition through virtual "shout-outs" or acknowledgment boards.
   - Highlight how collaborative efforts contributed to team successes.

8. Break Down Barriers to Speaking Up

   Application to Virtual Teams: Virtual teams often struggle with power dynamics and perceived barriers to open communication. Leaders must actively address these issues.

   - Create opportunities for anonymous feedback or suggestions.
   - Regularly invite junior team members to share their perspectives during virtual meetings.
   - Reward and recognize constructive dissent or alternative viewpoints.

9. Build Reflection into Team Processes

   Application to Virtual Teams: Without informal office interactions, virtual teams need structured opportunities for reflection to learn and improve.

   - Conduct regular retrospectives after projects to discuss lessons learned.
   - Use tools like SWOT analysis to evaluate team performance and relationships.
   - Share insights from reflections in a centralized online repository for future reference.

10. Establish Clear Boundaries and Accountability

    Application to Virtual Teams: Ambiguity in roles and expectations can exacerbate misunderstandings in virtual settings. Clear boundaries and accountability are critical.

    - Define roles and responsibilities explicitly at the start of projects.
    - Collaboratively establish virtual "rules of engagement" for communication and interactions.
    - Follow up on commitments to maintain trust and dependability.

CASE STUDY 1: THE TOUR DE FRANCE DOPING SCANDAL—CONFORMITY, AUTHORITY, AND THE NEED TO BELONG

In a stark, clinical room, a young cyclist sits nervously on the edge of a chair. Opposite him, a doctor in a pristine white coat holds up a small, hermetically sealed glass container, its contents glistening in the fluorescent light.

"This," the doctor says, tapping the container lightly, "is what it takes. You've worked hard to get here, but this is how champions are made." His tone is professional and confident. There is a sense that he's offering a gift, a secret potion that must be handled with great care. The cyclist shifts uncomfortably, "But … is this really necessary?"

The doctor smiles reassuringly, "I understand," he replies. "But you've earned this. Trust me, this is safe and everyone who succeeds has taken this step. And remember it's not just for your success—it's for the team, for the future."

The argument that this is for the greater good is the clincher and young cyclist's resistance is overcome. The syringe is prepared. The precious liquid is administered.

It sounds like something straight out of one of Stanley Milgram's famous obedience studies: a reluctant participant, a figure of authority (who in fact had no medical qualifications or training), and an act that overcomes personal conviction. But this is no psychological experiment. This was a real-life event that occurred in 1980, in the early days of the infamous drug-taking culture that plagued professional cycling and culminated in the Tour de France doping scandal. The "doctor" Bernard Sainz and the young cyclist René Wenzel were in a grim system that demanded success at any price, even if it involved cheating.

The doping scandal that engulfed the Tour de France, as detailed in David Walsh's books *From Lance to Landis*[15] and *Seven Deadly Sins*,[16] exposed a deeply entrenched culture of conformity, obedience to authority, together with a deep-seated need to belong to the team. It is a real-life example of group conformity, the power of authority, and groupthink, which reveals how these psychological and organizational mechanisms enabled the doping culture to thrive. First, it is necessary to outline the scandal itself, its buildup, and how it unfolded.

THE SCANDAL: A COLLAPSE OF INTEGRITY

The Tour de France doping scandal revealed a sophisticated, systematic, and deeply entrenched culture of performance-enhancing drug use within professional cycling. At its heart was Lance Armstrong, who recovered from cancer to win the Tour de France seven times from 1999 to 2005. Recognized as a hero, his story was a celebration of resilience, hope, and triumph. However, behind the scenes, Armstrong's success was achieved by a carefully coordinated doping program that involved his team, the complicity of cycling's governing bodies, and a culture of silence enforced through intimidation.

The run-up to the scandal began in the 1990s when the use of erythropoietin (EPO) became widespread in professional cycling. EPO, which enhances oxygen-carrying capacity by increasing the red blood cell count, provided a significant performance advantage, especially in endurance sports like cycling. Walsh's accounts describe how teams developed sophisticated methods to evade detection, including micro-dosing and manipulating blood tests to keep red blood cell count within acceptable hematocrit levels, which measure the percentage of red blood cells in the blood. The culture of doping became so pervasive that clean riders were effectively pushed out of the sport, unable to compete on a level playing field.

The scandal's public unraveling began with the Festina affair in 1998, when one of the team's support members, or soigneur, was caught with a car full of performance-enhancing drugs. This incident exposed the extent of doping in the sport but failed to bring about meaningful reform. By the time Armstrong began dominating the Tour de France in the early 2000s, doping had become an open secret, but due to the sophistication of the methods to avoid drug detection, there was no concrete evidence.

The tipping point came in 2012 when the United States Anti-Doping Agency (USADA) released a report detailing Armstrong's doping activities. The report included testimonies from teammates who described how Armstrong and team officials pressured them to participate in doping. The fallout was swift: Armstrong was stripped of his seven Tour de France titles, banned from professional cycling, and widely condemned for his role in perpetuating the doping culture.

CONFORMITY AND THE NEED TO BELONG

Social Pressures to Conform

Professional cycling teams during the era of widespread doping functioned as highly cohesive units, where the pressure to conform was intense. Riders operated in their own insular world where adherence to group norms was essential for survival. Doping became a tacit requirement for being part of the team. Riders who refused to dope, such as Christophe Bassons, faced ostracism and hostility from their peers. Bassons's decision to speak out against doping in 1999 was met with accusations of betrayal.

The need to belong to the team often overrode individual ethical considerations. Riders feared being labeled as "outsiders" or "troublemakers," knowing that such labels could jeopardize their careers. This reflects Irving Janis's observation that members of highly cohesive groups often suppress dissent to preserve group harmony.

The Role of Peer Reinforcement

Within teams, doping was not framed as an individual decision but as a collective necessity. Riders were expected to "do what it takes" to compete at the highest level, creating a shared understanding that doping was essential. This group mentality reinforced the behavior, as riders saw their teammates engaging in doping without facing immediate consequences. Walsh's depiction of the peloton's reaction to Bassons's resistance—including his own team's hostility—illustrates how peer reinforcement perpetuated the culture.

Riders who may have been uncomfortable with doping likely chose to conform because they perceived unanimous agreement within the group, even if that agreement was illusory.

The Fear of Isolation

Conformity was further driven by the fear of isolation. Riders who resisted doping faced social exclusion and professional marginalization. Walsh recounts how Bassons was excluded from team meetings and subjected to bullying by his peers. The psychological toll of this isolation eventually led him to abandon the Tour. This mirrors Janis's observation that members of cohesive groups fear being ostracized and will often conform to avoid being cast out.

The fear of isolation also extended to journalists and officials who dared to question the system. Walsh himself faced professional marginalization for his investigative work, illustrating how the broader cycling community enforced conformity not just among riders but across all stakeholders.

The Power of Leadership

We can't overlook Lance Armstrong's dominance over his team, which shows how authority figures can shape group behavior. Armstrong wielded immense power within the peloton, both as a leader and as a symbol of success. His teammates were expected to follow his lead, both on and off the bike. Walsh describes how Armstrong used intimidation and manipulation to ensure compliance, famously telling Bassons, "*If that's what you're here for, it would be better if you returned home and found some other kind of work.*"

Armstrong's leadership created a hierarchical structure where dissent was not tolerated. Riders who questioned the doping culture risked not only their place on the team but also their professional reputations. This reflects Stanley Milgram's findings on obedience to authority, where individuals comply with orders from authoritative figures even when those orders conflict with their personal ethics. Armstrong's status as a team leader and cycling icon amplified his authority, making it even more difficult for riders to resist. But it is also a demonstration of how powerful, charismatic individuals can exert undue influence in a team if they are not held accountable to ethical standards.

This shows how a lack of psychological safety means that individuals and teams connect in ways that are highly unethical.

In the next case study, we can see how psychological safety enables a team to produce outstanding, unconventional results.

CASE STUDY 2: THE MAKING OF *THE GODFATHER*

SCREENPLAY TITLE: *LEAVE THE GUN, TAKE THE CANNOLI: THE MAKING OF THE GODFATHER*

Scene 1

INTERIOR. PARAMOUNT OFFICES, NEW YORK CITY—JANUARY 25, 1971—DAY
The Gulf + Western Building. FRANCIS FORD COPPOLA, early 30s, sits across from a table of seasoned experts. He's passionate but visibly young compared to DEAN TAVOULARIS (production designer), GORDON WILLIS (cinematographer), and ANNA HILL "JOHNNIE" JOHNSTONE (costume designer).

COPPOLA
I want this film to be operatic. A clash of light and shadow, good and evil … but in every frame. We're not making just a movie—we're building an experience.

TAVOULARIS
(with a smile)
   Then the style has to be woven into every detail. Don't pan or cut much. Let the frame live on its own.

WILLIS
(nodding thoughtfully)
   That'll make it more painterly. Hold the scene—people drift in, they drift out.

JOHNSTONE
(supportive)
   I see it. The visuals, the clothes … everything pulls us into that world. If we go too theatrical, it's gone.
   The room quiets for a moment, Coppola taking in their ideas.

COPPOLA
So, minimal movement. Everything essential to that world—but understated. We're not building the 1940s scene by scene. It's more of an impression, right?

WILLIS
Exactly. That's why muted colors work here: no bold primary colors, just earth tones, browns, and blacks. The camera takes in the bare bones and lets the scene do the rest.

Scene 2

INT. PARAMOUNT OFFICES—CONTINUOUS
They focus on the wedding scene, a pivotal part of the story.

COPPOLA
I want that wedding to feel huge, a fusion of family and business. Don Corleone's office should never feel isolated from the celebration.

WILLIS

(suggesting)

What if we track from the wedding straight into his office, blending the two? And it's 1945—doors and windows wide open; no air conditioning back then.

JOHNSTONE

We will need waiters. Do you think ten would be enough or would there be more?

COPPOLA

There would be no waitstaff. It'd be the women doing it all, making sandwiches, pouring wine from barrels that had been given to them.

TAVOULARIS

Family and community—not hired staff. Don't forget those big straw-wrapped bottles.

COPPOLA

This feels good and real.

Scene 3

INT. PARAMOUNT OFFICES—BLOOD EFFECTS DISCUSSION

The conversation turns to realism in the film's violent scenes. Coppola is animated, but Willis is already thinking technically.

COPPOLA

We need the blood to look real—dark, a little congealed. Can we use real blood?

TAVOULARIS
Real blood would coagulate. It won't work for continuity.

WILLIS
(pauses, thinking)
  We can create a mixture that soaks like blood but congeals naturally. That'll hold up on camera.

COPPOLA
(grinning)
  Perfect.

Scene 4

INT. PARAMOUNT OFFICES—WRAPPING UP
The team is wrapping up. Coppola looks at each of them, clearly moved.

COPPOLA
Thank you, all of you. We're creating a piece of art here. Every detail matters.

JOHNSTONE
(supportively)
  We're in it together, Francis. One frame at a time.

WILLIS
(smiling, confident)
  Let's do it right. We're on the same page.
  They exchange nods, a shared determination to bring this vision to life.

FADE OUT

The making of *The Godfather* is a testament to the power of psychological safety in creative collaboration, which my attempt at a screenplay hopefully conveys. In the intense environment of the Paramount offices in January 1971, director Francis Ford Coppola and his team created a culture that allowed every member to voice ideas, challenge assumptions, and ultimately transform a gangster movie into an epic, operatic film masterpiece. Remarkably, we know what took place because Coppola had a stenographer who recorded every statement that each person made.

These conversations, and much more, are reported in the wonderful book *Leave the Gun, Take the Cannoli: The Making of the Godfather*[17] Psychological safety—the sense that individuals can speak their minds, contribute freely, and take risks without fear of negative repercussions—was essential to *The Godfather*'s creation. Coppola's youthful vision, paired with the expertise of his seasoned team, generated a dynamic where innovation and criticism were not only welcomed but essential. Through this creative environment, *The Godfather* became a film that not only redefined the crime genre but also deeply influenced American cinema.

COPPOLA'S VISION AND RESPECT FOR EXPERTISE

At the core of this collaborative success was Coppola's balance of vision and humility. Although Coppola had a clear direction for *The Godfather*, he was young and untested, particularly in comparison to his more experienced team. The film studio making the movie, Paramount Studios, was down on its luck and desperate for a financial blockbuster. They didn't trust the inexperienced Coppola, fearing that he was more concerned about making art than generating revenue. Furthermore, he was the eighth choice for the movie, with seven other far more accomplished directors having turned the project down.

Production designer Dean Tavoularis, cinematographer Gordon Willis, and costume designer Anna Hill "Johnnie" Johnstone each brought years of experience and their own unique insights to the project. Despite his relative inexperience, Coppola established a collaborative tone where everyone's input was valued. He didn't merely dictate his ideas; he encouraged the team to examine every aspect of the film in meticulous detail and empowered them to challenge his concepts if they saw room for improvement.

Coppola's approach exemplifies one of the key elements of psychological safety: a leader who values diverse perspectives and is willing to set aside their own ideas for better ones. This openness demonstrated to the team that Coppola respected their expertise, which, in turn, encouraged them to share ideas freely. Coppola's acknowledgment that he was learning as he went also fostered an environment where each member felt essential to the process, and their expertise elevated his vision.

Listening to the Contributions of the Whole Team

Psychological safety is built on trust and the freedom to express dissent, and this was evident in *The Godfather*'s production team. Gordon Willis, known as the "Prince of Darkness" for his mastery of shadow and sparse lighting, disagreed with Coppola on certain visual elements but felt empowered to share his opinions. Coppola took his advice, knowing that Willis's expertise would serve the film's atmosphere better than his initial ideas. The contrasts between light and darkness became essential to the visual storytelling of *The Godfather*, enhancing its themes of morality and family loyalty.

Similarly, Tavoularis contributed ideas that challenged traditional Hollywood depictions of the Italian-American crime family. Coppola's willingness to listen to these details allowed team members to focus on authenticity and artistry rather than merely adhering to genre conventions.

Encouraging Risk-Taking and Unconventional Ideas

Coppola's collaborative spirit encouraged the team to take risks that other directors might have dismissed. One significant decision was the team's treatment of violence and how it would be visually represented. Rather than showing violence as a series of sensationalized, choreographed sequences, Willis and Coppola agreed to let the brutality unfold in unsettling ways, often in broad daylight, which ran counter to the typical night settings of crime dramas. One of the many iconic scenes is the assassination of Paulie Gatto. The accepted and formulaic way of doing this would've been to focus on the actual shooting. Instead, Willis suggested that the camera should be focused somewhere else, letting the audience hear but not see the violence (at the conclusion of the scene, Clemenza, the gangster in charge of this operation, issues the famous words "leave the gun and take the cannoli"). This method of framing the violence made it feel almost incidental and more shocking as a result.

Attention to Detail and Shared Ownership

An essential benefit of psychological safety in any creative team is the enhanced attention to detail that results from a sense of shared ownership. For *The Godfather*'s production, no detail was too small for discussion, from the wedding banquet food to the look of the blood used in the violent scenes.

Additionally, Johnstone's meticulous work on costuming helped create a believable setting for 1945, down to Michael Corleone's military uniform and the understated attire of the Corleone family.

Without this level of granular attention to authenticity, *The Godfather* could have felt like just another gangster movie with exaggerated costumes and exaggerated violence. Instead, the team's collective eye for detail gave the film a sense of realism, allowing audiences to connect emotionally with the characters and the story.

FROM GANGSTER MOVIE TO MASTERPIECE

The production team, under Coppola's leadership, brought both innovation and restraint to the project, crafting a story that resonated on a profound, almost mythic level. Each member was allowed to play to their strengths and bring ideas to the table that subverted Hollywood norms, and each idea strengthened the film. Because the team felt empowered to take creative risks, question decisions, and focus on authenticity, *The Godfather* became more than a tale of crime—it became an exploration of power, loyalty, and identity.

One factor that the transcripts do not demonstrate is the way Coppola protected his team once filming began. He was under enormous pressure to comply with the demands of the studio, as well as the expectations of the Hollywood system to produce a gangster movie that conformed to the rules of the genre. Instead of showing the stress that he was experiencing, he stuck to his vision and enabled the team to participate fully in order to achieve it.

Without psychological safety, such unconventional approaches might have been dismissed as too subtle or confusing. However, because the team felt encouraged to take creative risks, they created a style that set *The Godfather* apart from other crime films. Ultimately, psychological safety transformed *The Godfather* from a genre piece into a cinematic masterpiece.

KEY POINTS

It's important not to underestimate the power of wanting to belong to a team and not to stand out. Solomon Asch's classic studies revealed that this desire can lead us to suppress our points of view in order to conform to the majority opinion in the group. This means that dissenting views are less likely to be aired, robbing a group of alternative perspectives, which may add to, or even change, the decisions that are taken.

Fostering psychological safety within teams is essential for their success as well as the engagement and well-being of team members. The pioneering work of Amy Edmondson demonstrates the powerful results that are obtained when psychological safety exists. Google's Project Aristotle further confirmed Edmondson's insights.

Ten principles for creating psychological safety in teams were provided based on Amy Edmondson's work. These principles can be applied to more traditional, face-to-face teams, but also to virtual and remote teams. One of the important lessons from Project Aristotle was that psychological safety was more important than where a team was located.

The Tour de France doping scandal is a powerful cautionary tale about how deeply entrenched cultural norms, unchecked authority, and the absence of psychological safety can lead to ethical collapse.

The making of the *The Godfather*, however, reveals, due to the foresight of Francis Ford Coppola in having meetings recorded for posterity, that great work can be created when psychological safety exists for the team members.

GLOSSARY

Conformity. The act of aligning one's behavior, beliefs, or opinions with those of a group, often due to social pressure. In Solomon Asch's experiments, individuals faced a choice between their own perceptions and the majority's incorrect views.

Conformity arises for several reasons:

- Doubt in one's own judgment, assuming the group must be right.
- A desire to maintain harmony and avoid conflict.
- Fear of appearing foolish or difficult.

Not everyone conformed; around 25% consistently resisted group pressure, showing confidence in their judgment and a sense of duty to uphold the truth.

NOTES

1 Asch, S.E. (1955). Opinions and social pressure. *Scientific American*, 193(5), pp. 31–35.

2 Abrams, D. & Levine, J.M. (2012). The formation of social norms: Revisiting Sherif's autokinetic illusion study. In: S. Hogg and J.M. Levine, eds. Social Psychology: Revisiting the Classic Studies. London: SAGE, pp. 57–75. Available at: https://www.researchgate.net/publication/314120328_The_formation_of_social_norms_Revisiting_Sherif's_autokinetic_illusion_study [Accessed 10 July 2025].

3 Bond, R. & Smith, P.B. (1996). Culture and conformity: A meta-analysis of studies using Asch's (1952b, 1956) line judgment task. *Psychological Bulletin*, 119(1), p. 111.

4 Usto Muamer, Drace Sasa, & Hadziahmetovic Nina (2019): Replication of the "Asch Effect" in Bosnia and Herzegovina: Evidence for the moderating role of group similarity in conformity. *Psychological Topics*, 28, pp. 589–599.

5 Mori, K. & Arai, M. (2010). No need to fake it: Reproduction of the Asch experiment without confederates. *International Journal of Psychology*, 45(5), pp. 390–397.

6 Takano, Yohtaro & Sogon, Shunya (2008). Are Japanese more collectivistic than Americans? Examining conformity in in-groups and the reference-group effect. *Journal of Cross-Cultural Psychology*, 39, pp. 237–250.

7 Franzen, A. & Mader, S. (2023). The power of social influence: A replication and extension of the Asch experiment. *PLOS ONE*, 18(11), p. e0294325.

8 Duhigg, C. (2016). What Google learned from its quest to build the perfect team. *New York Times Magazine*, 26, p. 2016.

9 Wu, P.P.Y., Babaei, T., O'Shea, M., Mengersen, K., Drovandi, C., McGibbon, K.E., Pyne, D.B., Mitchell, L.J., & Osborne, M.A. (2021). Predicting performance in 4 x 200-m freestyle swimming relay events. *PLOS ONE*, 16(7), p.e0254538.

10 Lechner, A. & Tobias Mortlock, J.M. (2022). How to create psychological safety in virtual teams. *Organizational Dynamics*, 51(2).

11 Sjöblom, K., Mäkiniemi, J.P., & Mäkikangas, A. (2022). "I was given three marks and told to buy a porsche"—supervisors' experiences of leading psychosocial safety climate and team psychological safety in a

remote academic setting. *International Journal of Environmental Research and Public Health*, *19*(19), p. 12016.

12 Lechner, A. & Tobias Mortlock, J.M. (2022). How to create psychological safety in virtual teams. *Organizational Dynamics*, *51*(2).

13 Lechner, A. & Tobias Mortlock, J.M. (2022). How to create psychological safety in virtual teams. *Organizational Dynamics*, *51*(2).

14 Sjöblom, K., Mäkiniemi, J.P. & Mäkikangas, A. (2022). "I was given three marks and told to buy a porsche"—supervisors' experiences of leading psychosocial safety climate and team psychological safety in a remote academic setting. *International Journal of Environmental Research and Public Health*, *19*(19), p. 12016.

15 Walsh, D. (2007). *From Lance to Landis: Inside the American Doping Controversy at the Tour de France*. Ballantine Books.

16 Walsh, D. (2013). *Seven Deadly Sins: My Pursuit of Lance Armstrong*. Simon & Schuster.

17 Seal, M. (2021). *Leave the Gun, Take the Cannoli: The Epic Story of the Making of The Godfather*. New York: Gallery Books.

FURTHER READING

Asch, S.E., 1955. Opinions and social pressure. *Scientific American*, 193(5), pp. 31–35.

Duhigg, C., 2016, February 26. What Google learned from its quest to build the perfect team. *The New York Times Magazine*.

Seal, M., 2021. *Leave the gun, take the cannoli: The epic story of the making of the godfather*. Gallery Books.

Video: "What Google Learned from Its Quest to Build the Perfect Team" – https://www.youtube.com/watch?v=hHIikHJV9fI

7

WHAT IS THE ROLE OF
THE INDIVIDUAL?

INTRODUCTION

The Stanford Prison Experiment (SPE), conducted by psychologist Philip Zimbardo in 1971, is one of the most unsettling demonstrations of how environments can drive ordinary people to extraordinary extremes.[1] What was intended to be an experiment within the controlled environment of an academic study rapidly led to a psychological breakdown of identity, ethics, and empathy. The SPE serves as a sobering reminder of how psychological safety can collapse when individuals are so immersed in their roles that they behave in ways that they understand to be expected of them. It revealed how people can be persuaded to behave in ways that would otherwise be unthinkable, to not challenge unethical behavior, and to brush aside anyone who criticizes them in order to justify what they carried out. The study reveals all of these things—only not in the way you may have thought.

This chapter delves into the role of the individual within such contexts, exploring how psychological safety can be upheld or compromised based on the intricate interplay between personal values, social norms, and systemic pressures. The second part of this chapter explores the critical role of bystanders and emphasizes how, both as individuals and as part of a collective, we can actively

DOI: 10.4324/9781003501855-9

foster psychological safety by taking effective action against unacceptable behavior.

THE STANFORD PRISON EXPERIMENT: A FAMILIAR STORY

In 1971, Stanford University's Philip Zimbardo carried out one of psychology's most famous and controversial studies. Known as the Stanford Prison Experiment (SPE), it was designed to explore the psychological effects of perceived power. The experiment involved 24 male college students who were randomly assigned roles as either guards or prisoners in a simulated prison environment. The setup appeared straightforward but yielded results that have been discussed and debated for decades.

Participants were chosen based on their psychological health and absence of criminal history. The basement of Stanford's Psychology Department was converted into a mock prison, complete with cells, uniforms, and guards equipped with batons and mirrored sunglasses to mask their eyes. Prisoners were stripped of individuality, referred to only by numbers, and dressed in degrading smocks. The guards, in contrast, were given authority over the prisoners and told to maintain order.

Over six days, the behavior of the participants escalated alarmingly. Guards imposed increasingly harsh punishments, including forced physical exercise, humiliation, and solitary confinement. Some guards exhibited overtly sadistic tendencies, while others passively went along with the abusive norms. The prisoners, meanwhile, became submissive and compliant, with some showing signs of severe psychological distress. One prisoner, known as "8612," reportedly suffered an emotional breakdown and was released early. Acts of resistance were rare and were discouraged by both the guards and other prisoners.

The experiment, originally scheduled to last two weeks, was terminated after just six days when Christina Maslach, a visiting researcher, objected to the inhumane treatment she observed.

Zimbardo's role as both the researcher and the prison superintendent blurred the lines of objectivity, raising ethical questions that persist to this day.

WHAT THIS SHOWS ABOUT HUMAN BEHAVIOR

Traditionally, the SPE has been interpreted as a stark demonstration of the power of situational forces. It is seen as evidence that people conform to roles when placed in hierarchical systems, abandoning their individual morality to meet perceived expectations. The guards' cruelty has been linked to the corrupting influence of power, while the prisoners' compliance is seen as an example of obedience to authority and the suppression of dissent.

The SPE has been used to explain real-world atrocities, from the Holocaust to Abu Ghraib, suggesting that ordinary individuals, under the right conditions, can be led to commit extraordinary acts of cruelty. It has also highlighted the dangers of unchecked power and the dehumanization of others within structured systems.

All of this paints a dark and disturbing picture of human nature, I'm sure you would agree. Except that … it didn't happen like this. The truly dark and disturbing behavior in the Stanford Prison Experiment wasn't confined to the guards or prisoners; it was orchestrated and reinforced by the experimenters themselves. Let's retell the story based on what we now know and explore what this means for individual responsibility and psychological safety.

A TWIST IN THE TALE: THE EXPERIMENTERS' ROLE IN THE SPE

Recent analyses by scholars such as Haslam et al.,[2] Bartels and Griggs,[3] and Le Texier[4] reveal that the traditional narrative of the SPE is deeply flawed. Far from being a natural demonstration of role conformity, the behaviors exhibited by participants were significantly influenced—if not outright directed—by the experimenters.

Experimenters' Direct Influence and Leadership

The guards' abusive behavior was not spontaneous. Archival materials show that Philip Zimbardo and his team provided explicit instructions during a pre-experiment orientation session. Guards were told to instill fear, enforce arbitrary rules, and strip prisoners of their individuality. Zimbardo himself reportedly stated, "We can create boredom. We can create a sense of frustration. We can create fear in them … In general, what all this should create in them is a sense of powerlessness."[5]

This direct guidance undermines the claim that the guards' actions emerged naturally from the dynamics of the situation. Instead, the guards were following the experimenters' cues, acting out roles that had been deliberately outlined for them. This is an example of identity leadership, where leaders shape group norms and behaviors by framing them as aligned with a shared mission or purpose. Zimbardo positioned himself as part of the guards' in-group, aligning their actions with the supposed scientific goals of the study.[6]

Demand Characteristics and Acting

The participants were not merely reacting to the situation; they were responding to perceived expectations. Many guards later admitted that they were "acting" to fulfill what they believed the researchers wanted. Similarly, the prisoners were manipulated into believing they could not leave the experiment, creating a feeling of entrapment. The staging of the experiment and the expectations, or demand characteristics, it engendered was something that Zimbardo would strongly resist and refute in the years that followed.[7]

Participants' Failure to Speak Up

A striking aspect of the SPE is the lack of dissent, not only among the guards and prisoners but also among the participants as a whole.

Even those who were uncomfortable with the escalating cruelty did not speak out against the researchers. This failure to challenge authority highlights a broader issue: how individuals, even in positions to act, can feel powerless in hierarchical systems.

Several factors contributed to this silence:

1. **Authority and Leadership**: Zimbardo's dual role as researcher and superintendent reinforced his authority, making participants reluctant to question his directives.
2. **Group Dynamics**: Guards who were uncomfortable with the abuse likely felt isolated and feared breaking group cohesion by speaking out.
3. **Psychological Safety for Compliance, Not Dissent**: The guards experienced psychological safety to conform to expectations but not to challenge them. The prisoners, stripped of agency, were in no position to dissent. However, the prisoners had been conditioned by the experimenters as to their role in the study. Despite Zimbardo's insistence that the prisoners could leave at any point, the archival material shows that they were informed there was very little chance of them leaving unless there was illness or a special authorization given to them by the experimenters.[8]

This lack of resistance reveals a critical vulnerability in human behavior: when individuals perceive authority as legitimate, they are less likely to challenge unethical norms, even when they recognize them as wrong.

LESSONS FOR INDIVIDUAL RESPONSIBILITY AND PSYCHOLOGICAL SAFETY

The SPE, when retold with these revelations, shifts from being a study about role conformity to a cautionary tale about leadership, authority, and individual responsibility. Despite its flaws, the experiment offers valuable lessons for understanding psychological safety and the conditions that encourage or suppress ethical behavior, except not in the way that the experiment has always suggested.

Psychological Safety Requires Ethical Leadership

Zimbardo's leadership fostered psychological safety for guards to explore abusive behaviors without fear of judgment or consequences. Protection was provided further by framing harmful behavior as essential for achieving the study's goals. True psychological safety must include an ethical framework that prioritizes accountability and mutual respect.

For organizations, this highlights the need for leaders to model ethical behavior and create environments where individuals feel safe to question harmful norms. Leaders must explicitly encourage questioning, if not dissent and protect those who raise concerns.

The Power of Individual Responsibility

The failure of participants to speak out against the experimenters highlights the importance of individual responsibility. Even in hierarchical systems, individuals have the capacity to challenge unethical behavior. However, doing so requires courage and a supportive environment.

Organizations can foster this by:

- Training employees to recognize and address unethical practices.
- Establishing clear channels for reporting concerns without fear of retaliation.
- Celebrating instances where individuals take a stand reinforces the value of ethical behavior.

Psychological Safety Is Not About Compliance

In the SPE, the guards conformed to expectations because they felt "safe" within their roles. However, this form of safety suppressed ethical accountability. Psychological safety should not equate to an absence of consequences for harmful actions. Instead, it should empower individuals to act ethically, even when it requires breaking group norms.

Recognizing and Challenging Power Dynamics

The SPE demonstrates how power dynamics can suppress dissent and perpetuate harmful behaviors. Participants who felt uncomfortable with the cruelty may have feared challenging Zimbardo's authority or breaking group cohesion. Recognizing these dynamics is essential for creating environments where individuals feel empowered to act.

Organizations must actively address power imbalances by:

- Encouraging transparency and open communication.
- Providing training on the influence of authority and group dynamics.
- Ensuring that leaders are held accountable for fostering ethical behavior.

Balancing Group Norms and Individual Agency

The SPE reveals the dangers of prioritizing group norms over individual agency. While norms provide structure and cohesion, they can also suppress critical thinking and ethical judgment. Encouraging diversity of thought and creating space for dissent can help mitigate these risks.

Recognizing the Ways People are Led to Unethical Behavior

In *The Lucifer Effect*, Zimbardo outlines ten psychological strategies that are often employed to lead individuals toward unethical behavior. These methods create environments conducive to compliance and diminish resistance. I present these strategies below because I believe they have value for people in organizations to identify when they are being manipulated. These same strategies were used, perhaps cynically, in Zimbardo's Stanford Prison Experiment, to influence participants' behavior:

1. **Contractual Obligation**: Zimbardo used verbal agreements, where participants signed up to participate in a prison study. While they knew they could technically leave, the language used by experimenters often suggested otherwise, making participants feel legally bound to stay.
2. **Meaningful Roles**: Participants were assigned roles as "guards" and "prisoners." These roles carried with them societal associations—guards were expected to be authoritative, and prisoners were seen as submissive. These learned behaviors became the foundation of their actions during the experiment.
3. **Basic Rules and Justification**: Experimenters established a framework of rules that seemed logical initially (e.g., maintaining order) but were later used arbitrarily to justify oppressive behaviors. Guards followed these rules without questioning their fairness or necessity.
4. **Semantic Reframing**: The rhetoric used by experimenters reframed unethical actions as part of a greater good. For instance, guards were told their actions were necessary for the "study of human behavior" and for understanding the dynamics of imprisonment. This replaced the reality of harm with a "scientific" justification.
5. **Diffusion of Responsibility**: Zimbardo minimized participants' sense of individual accountability. Guards believed their actions were part of a group effort or directly encouraged by the experimenter. As a result, participants felt less personally responsible for unethical behavior.
6. **Initial Small Steps**: The experiment began with minor exercises of power—such as guards enforcing prisoners' compliance with rules—creating a "foot in the door" phenomenon.

These small actions escalated into more extreme measures, such as humiliation and solitary confinement.

7. **Gradual Escalation**: The abuse increased incrementally. Guards started with mild discipline but gradually introduced harsher punishments, such as forced exercises or denial of basic needs. Each new step felt like a logical continuation of the last.

8. **Changing Authority Dynamics**: Initially, Zimbardo presented himself as a neutral observer, but as the experiment progressed, his role as "prison superintendent" became more prominent. This shift confused participants, who were unsure whether he was a researcher or an authority figure enforcing rules.

9. **High Exit Costs**: Though participants technically had the right to leave, Zimbardo made it difficult for prisoners to exit. Guards were implicitly pressured to stay committed to their roles, fearing they would let down the experiment if they failed to comply. The students also took part in the experiment because they were being paid and wanted to receive their payment for their participation.

10. **Ideology and Justification**: Zimbardo presented the experiment as an important scientific endeavor to study the psychology of imprisonment. This "big lie" allowed participants to rationalize their unethical actions as contributions to a noble cause.

CONCLUSION

The Stanford Prison Experiment, when revisited through the lens of modern critiques, shifts from being a story about the power of people's roles to a lesson in leadership, authority, and the suppression of dissent. It demonstrates how psychological safety can be weaponized to reinforce harmful norms and how the absence of ethical oversight enables destructive behavior.

The ultimate lesson is clear: psychological safety is not just about feeling secure but about fostering an environment where

Table 7.1 *Applying the Ten Steps of Persuading People to Unethical Behavior to the SPE*

Method	Description	Application in the SPE
1. Contractual obligation	Creating a sense of obligation through verbal or written agreements	Participants believed they were obligated to stay, despite their right to withdraw
2. Meaningful roles	Assigning roles with associated positive societal values	Roles of "guards" and "prisoners" activated learned behaviors of authority and submission
3. Basic rules and justification	Establishing rules that initially seem fair, but become tools for oppression	Guards used rules arbitrarily to control prisoners, justifying their actions as necessary for maintaining order
4. Semantic reframing	Replacing unpleasant, realities with desirable rhetoric	Harmful actions were refrained as contributions to scientific research, masking their ethical implications
5. Diffusion of responsibility	Reducing individual accountability by spreading responsibility	Guards saw their actions as following orders, or as part of a group effort, minimizing personal guilt
6. Initial small steps	Starting with minor actions that escalate over time	Guards began with minor enforcement, leading to more extreme acts of punishment and humiliation
7. Gradual escalation	Gradually increasing the severity of actions	The progression from minor discipline to psychological abuse and deprivation made each step seem acceptable
8. Changing authority dynamics	Transforming authority, figures from neutral to demanding	Zimbardo's shift from researcher to "prison, superintendent" confused, participants, and reinforced compliance with unethical acts

(Continued)

Table 7.1 (Continued)

Method	Description	Application in the SPE
9. High exit costs	Making it difficult or costly for individuals to leave	Prisoners were discouraged from leaving, and guards felt compelled to continue their roles to support the study's goals
10. Ideology and justification	Offering a noble cause to rationalize unethical behavior	The experiments framing as important psychological research justified, participants, harmful actions

individuals feel empowered to take ethical action, question authority, and hold both themselves and others accountable. Only in such an environment can true integrity and accountability flourish.

BYSTANDER BEHAVIORS

Here is the headline story from the *New York Times* in 1964:

37 Who Saw Murder Didn't Call the Police

For more than half an hour 38 respectable, law-abiding citizens in Queens watched a killer stalk and stab a woman in three separate attacks in Kew Gardens.

Twice the sound of their voices and the sudden glow of their bedroom lights interrupted him and frightened him off. Each time he returned, sought her out and stabbed her again. Not one person telephoned the police during the assault; one witness called after the woman was dead.

That was two weeks ago today. But Assistant Chief Inspector Frederick M. Lussen, in charge of the borough's detectives and a veteran of 25 years of homicide investigations, is still shocked.

He can give a matter-of-fact recitation of many murders. But the Kew Gardens slaying baffles him—not because it is a murder, but because the "good people" failed to call the police.[9]

The story of Kitty Genovese's murder in 1964 has become a defining example in discussions of bystander behavior and public apathy. According to the original *New York Times* article by Martin Gansberg, 38 witnesses watched from their windows as Genovese was brutally attacked in three separate incidents over half an hour, yet none called the police until after she was dead. This shocking narrative painted a disturbing picture of human indifference, influencing social psychology studies and theories on bystander inaction and crowd mentality. For decades, this story was used in textbooks and classrooms to demonstrate how people, particularly in groups, might fail to intervene in emergencies.

However, recent investigations have revealed that this narrative was more myth than reality. For instance, not all of the 38 witnesses were direct eyewitnesses; some only heard parts of the incident and were unclear about what was happening. Contrary to the story's portrayal, several residents did call the police, including one witness who called immediately after the first attack. Additionally, rather than three attacks, there were two, and the second took place inside a building, out of sight for most witnesses.[10]

Significantly, witnesses did, in fact, take action that disrupted the attack. Kitty's attacker, Winston Moseley, was scared off after the initial assault due to noise and light from nearby apartments. A resident, Sophie Farrar, also came to her aid during the second attack, staying with her in her final moments. The 911 centralized emergency system didn't exist at the time, so contacting the police was more difficult then, and, when they did get through, there were reports that residents' calls were met with skepticism.[11]

This revised understanding of the Genovese case has significant implications for the study and understanding of bystander behavior. While the story's initial portrayal might suggest that people are naturally indifferent to others' suffering, the reality is more nuanced. Many residents were unsure of what was happening, and some did attempt to intervene or alert authorities. Rather than indifference, this suggests that situational factors—like the clarity of the situation and the accessibility of emergency services—played a critical role in bystander responses.

Despite the way the Kitty Genovese story is related and perpetuated in books, most notably those on psychology, it nevertheless spurred research into bystander behavior, which has proven to be of great benefit. It helps us understand what bystander behavior is, how people choose to intervene, if at all, and the effectiveness of their actions. After all, at many points in our lives, all of us will be bystanders, so it is worth considering this in more detail here.

WHAT IS BYSTANDER BEHAVIOR?

The bystander effect is a psychological phenomenon in which an individual's likelihood of offering help decreases when other passive bystanders are present in a critical situation. Bibb Latané and John Darley first empirically demonstrated the bystander effect in a series of studies, showing that people are less likely to assist when in a group, assuming others will take responsibility or that their help isn't necessary. The research provides critical insights into human behavior in situations that call for intervention.[1213]

The bystander effect relates closely to the concept of psychological safety. In situations where psychological safety is high, individuals will feel more empowered to act, despite the presence of others. However, when psychological safety is low, the bystander effect is more likely to manifest, as individuals hesitate to take action, fearing judgment, embarrassment, or other social repercussions.

The work of Fischer and colleagues extended the exploration of the bystander effect by conducting a meta-analysis on bystander intervention in both dangerous and non-dangerous contexts.[14] There are a number of important observations and actionable insights that can be made from the research relating to:

- Group size and the diffusion of responsibility
- The perceived personal cost of intervention
- The impact of knowledge and awareness of the bystander effect
- The effect of social identity and shared group membership
- Ambiguity, pluralistic ignorance and social influence
- Moral intensity
- Role expectations and responsibility
- Modeling and observational learning
- Cost-benefit analysis
- Collective and coordinated intervention

Group size and diffusion of responsibility. Studies consistently show that as the number of bystanders increases, the likelihood of any one person intervening decreases. This effect, referred to earlier in this chapter and known as diffusion of responsibility, suggests that each individual in a group assumes someone else will step in. This has been observed not only in more dramatic situations, for example, involving theft, but also in every day and mundane events, such as helping someone who has dropped pencils in an elevator or tipping waiting staff in restaurants. When people dropped pencils in elevators, the likelihood of someone helping decreased with each additional person present. Similarly, diners in larger groups tipped less, each assuming others would cover the generosity.[15] These studies illustrate something which is central to understanding the bystander effect, namely how responsibility becomes diluted in groups.

The perceived personal cost of intervention plays a crucial role in influencing decisions to help. People are more likely to intervene when the potential cost of not helping is high for themselves. For example, in dangerous situations where there is a physical risk, bystanders may recognize that inaction could endanger themselves as well as the victim, prompting them to act. This finding suggests that intervention decisions are often driven by self-preservation rather than solely concern for the victim. By framing intervention as a way to mitigate personal risk, this insight can be used to design strategies that encourage bystanders to help.

Knowledge and awareness of the bystander effect itself also appear to reduce apathy. When people are aware of the bystander effect, they are more likely to intervene in situations requiring help. For instance, students who learned about the bystander effect were later more likely to take action in emergencies. This points to the importance of public awareness and education: teaching people about this phenomenon empowers them to recognize and counteract it in real life.

Social identity and shared group membership are other important factors in bystander behavior. Research shows that individuals are more likely to help someone they perceive as part of their in group, which could be based on shared characteristics or social identities.[16] In workplaces, fostering a sense of inclusion and highlighting shared values between different groups can enhance people's sense of responsibility toward each other, thereby promoting intervention in critical situations.

Ambiguity, pluralistic ignorance and social influence also affect whether people take action. In ambiguous situations, bystanders often look to others for cues, which can lead to inaction if no one else seems concerned. This phenomenon, known as pluralistic ignorance, occurs when we, as bystanders, interpret others' calm reactions as a signal that intervention is unnecessary.[17] Observers rely on the reactions of others, particularly those they perceive as similar, to determine whether a situation requires intervention.[18] What we don't realize is that the people I am looking at to determine how I should respond are also looking at me to decide how they will react.

In organizational or public settings, this can lead to passivity. Recognizing this, leaders and managers can take proactive steps by setting examples of intervention or encouraging direct communication in uncertain situations, which helps break the cycle of inaction.

Moral intensity is another factor that determines intervention likelihood. Situations perceived as morally intense are more likely to provoke intervention, as bystanders see these events as requiring action.[19] In cases of harassment, for example, if an observer does not view the event as morally pressing, they are less likely to intervene.[20] This insight suggests that organizations can benefit from establishing clear ethical standards and highlighting the moral implications of certain behaviors, thereby framing these situations as morally significant and deserving of intervention.

Role expectations and responsibility also influence intervention behavior—as we have seen in the Stanford Prison Experiment. Individuals in positions of authority, such as supervisors or human resources professionals, are more likely to intervene in cases of harassment or misconduct because they have formal responsibilities and may face legal consequences for inaction.[21] This shows the importance of clearly defining intervention responsibilities within organizations and creating policies that empower certain individuals to act when needed. It may also mean that others who could intervene choose not to because they don't see it as part of their responsibilities.

Modeling and observational learning play a powerful role in encouraging intervention. People who observe others taking action are more likely to act themselves, as seeing intervention in action reduces inhibitions and provides guidance on when and how to respond.[22] Training videos, stories of successful interventions, and real-life examples can effectively teach bystanders how to step in, lowering their reluctance and boosting confidence in responding to similar situations.

The cost–benefit analysis that observers conduct before intervening is a well-documented behavior in bystander research. Individuals often weigh the risks and benefits of intervening, especially in workplace or social environments with high-stakes consequences.[23] In cases of whistle-blowing, for instance, bystanders assess the potential backlash, such as strained relationships or retaliation, and may opt against intervention if the costs appear too high. This finding highlights the importance of creating supportive environments where individuals feel protected from negative repercussions for doing the right thing, thus reducing the perceived risks associated with intervention.

Collective and coordinated intervention can be more effective than individual action, particularly in violent or escalatory situations. Research shows that collective action from multiple individuals is more likely to result in a nonviolent resolution compared to interventions by a single person.[24] For instance, studies on conflict resolution reveal that violence is less likely to escalate when three separate bystanders step in, emphasizing the power of coordinated action.[25]

This is important in organizational settings. Where the cost–benefit analysis shows a high risk of someone intervening, this can be mitigated by more than one person coming forward together. First, the individuals in the group can support one another through the process. Second, the person who is being told is less likely to dismiss the feedback as merely the misinterpretation of events by one anxious individual. This insight can inform policies and training that promote teamwork in high-stakes situations, ensuring that individuals know they can rely on others for support.

The various factors identified through these studies demonstrate that bystander behavior is far from passive; it is influenced by social, psychological, and situational variables. These findings suggest that interventions aimed at countering the bystander effect should focus on fostering responsibility, promoting awareness, and creating supportive group dynamics.

By addressing these factors, organizations can encourage environments where people feel empowered and prepared to take action, reducing the bystander effect and encouraging supportive, proactive behavior in the face of critical situations.

CONCLUSION

Understanding the revised story of Kitty Genovese's murder allows us to consider how bystanders can play an active role in challenging harmful behaviors. Rather than being passive observers, bystanders have the power to disrupt potentially harmful situations by making their presence known, signaling for help, or intervening directly when it is safe to do so.

By recognizing their influence in-group settings, individuals can counteract the diffusion of responsibility and encourage others to step in. Social psychology thus encourages people to embrace their capacity for action, highlighting that bystander intervention can make a crucial difference in moments of crisis.

GLOSSARY

The bystander effect. A psychological phenomenon where the likelihood of an individual offering help decreases when other passive bystanders are present during a critical situation. First demonstrated by Bibb Latané and John Darley, the effect occurs because individuals often assume that someone else will take responsibility or believe their help isn't needed.

The Stanford Prison Experiment. A 1971 study by psychologist Philip Zimbardo that revealed how environments and assigned roles can drive people to extreme behaviors. Participants, assigned as either "guards" or "prisoners," quickly immersed themselves in their roles, leading to ethical breakdowns and cruelty. However, later analysis suggests that many of the participants were manipulated by experimenters, performing in ways they thought were expected of them. The SPE highlighted the dangers of the collapse of psychological safety and the ease with which unethical behavior can go unchallenged—but not in the traditional way often described.

NOTES

1 Zimbardo, Philip (2008). *The Lucifer Effect*. Random House.
2 Haslam, S.A., Reicher, S.D., & Van Bavel, J.J. (2019). Rethinking the nature of cruelty: The role of identity leadership in the Stanford Prison Experiment. American Psychologist, 74(7), p. 809.
3 Bartels, J.M. & Griggs, R.A. (2019). Using new revelations about the Stanford prison experiment to address APA undergraduate psychology major learning outcomes. S*cholarship of Teaching and Learning in Psychology*, 5(4), p. 298.
4 Le Texier, T. (2019). Debunking the Stanford Prison Experiment. *American Psychologist*, *74*(7), p. 823.
5 Haslam, S.A., Reicher, S.D., & Van Bavel, J.J. (2019). Rethinking the nature of cruelty: The role of identity leadership in the Stanford Prison Experiment. American Psychologist, 74(7), p. 809.
6 Le Texier, T. (2019). Debunking the Stanford Prison Experiment. *American Psychologist*, *74*(7), p. 823.
7 Bartels, J.M. & Griggs, R.A. (2019). Using new revelations about the Stanford prison experiment to address APA undergraduate psychology major learning outcomes. S*cholarship of Teaching and Learning in Psychology*, 5(4), p. 298.
8 Le Texier, T. (2019). Debunking the Stanford Prison Experiment. *American Psychologist*, *74*(7), p. 823.
9 Gansberg, M. (1964). 37 who saw murder didn't call the police. *New York Times*, 27.
10 Manning, R., Levine, M., & Collins, A. (2007). The Kitty Genovese murder and the social psychology of helping: The parable of the 38 witnesses. *American Psychologist*, *62*(6), p. 555.
11 Manning, R., Levine, M., & Collins, A. (2007). The Kitty Genovese murder and the social psychology of helping: The parable of the 38 witnesses. *American Psychologist*, 62(6), p. 555.
12 Darley, J.M. & Latané, B. (1968). Bystander intervention in emergencies: diffusion of responsibility. *Journal of Personality and Social Psychology*, *8*(4), p. 377.
13 Latané, B. and Darley, J.M. (1969). Bystander Apathy. American Scientist, *57*(2), pp. 244–268.
14 Fischer, P., Krueger, J.I., Greitemeyer, T., Vogrincic, C., Kastenmüller, A., Frey, D., Heene, M., Wicher, M., & Kainbacher, M. (2011). The

bystander-effect: a meta-analytic review on bystander intervention in dangerous and non-dangerous emergencies. *Psychological Bulletin*, *137*(4), p. 517.

15 Latané, B. & Nida, S. (1981). Ten years of research on group size and helping. *Psychological Bulletin*, *89*(2), p. 308.

16 Bowes-Sperry, L. & O'Leary-Kelly, A.M. (2005). To act or not to act: The dilemma faced by sexual harassment observers. Academy of Management Review, 30(2), pp. 288–306.

17 Latané, B. & Darley, J.M. (1970). Social determinants of bystander intervention in emergencies. In: J. Macauley and L. Berkowitz, eds. *Altruism and Helping Behavior.* New York: Academic Press, pp. 13–27.

18 Bowes-Sperry, L. & O'Leary-Kelly, A.M. (2005). To act or not to act: The dilemma faced by sexual harassment observers. Academy of Management Review, 30(2), pp. 288–306.

19 Bowes-Sperry, L. & O'Leary-Kelly, A.M. (2005). To act or not to act: The dilemma faced by sexual harassment observers. Academy of Management Review, *30*(2), pp. 288–306.

20 Bowes-Sperry, L. & O'Leary-Kelly, A.M. (2005). To act or not to act: The dilemma faced by sexual harassment observers. Academy of Management Review, 30(2), pp. 288–306.

21 Bowes-Sperry, L. & O'Leary-Kelly, A.M. (2005). To act or not to act: The dilemma faced by sexual harassment observers. Academy of Management Review, *30*(2), pp. 288–306.

22 Bandura, A. (1986). Social Foundations of Thought and Action: A Social Cognitive Theory. Englewood Cliffs, NJ: Prentice-Hall, pp. 23–28.

23 Bowes-Sperry, L. & O'Leary-Kelly, A.M. (2005). To act or not to act: The dilemma faced by sexual harassment observers. Academy of Management Review, *30*(2), pp. 288–306.

24 Levine, M., Taylor, P.J. & Best, R. (2011). Third parties, violence, and conflict resolution: The role of group size and collective action in the microregulation of violence. Psychological science, *22*(3), pp. 406–412.

25 Levine, M., Taylor, P.J., & Best, R. (2011). Third parties, violence, and conflict resolution: The role of group size and collective action in the microregulation of violence. *Psychological science*, *22*(3), pp. 406–412.

FURTHER READING

Darley, J.M. and Latané, B., 1968. Bystander intervention in emergencies: Diffusion of responsibility. *Journal of Personality and Social Psychology*, 8(4), pp. 377–383.

Le Texier, T., 2019. Debunking the Stanford prison experiment. *American Psychologist*, 74(7), p. 823.

Video: "The Bystander Effect Explained" – https://www.youtube.com/watch?v=OSsPfbup0ac

Zimbardo, P.G., 2008. *The lucifer effect: Understanding how good people turn evil.* Random House.

8

PSYCHOLOGICAL SAFETY:
BUT FOR WHO?

INTRODUCTION

Psychological safety has become a cornerstone concept in workplace dynamics, a vital ingredient for creativity, collaboration, and high performance. The question is often framed at the group level: Is this team psychologically safe? But this framing can obscure an important reality—that within a group that appears to enjoy psychological safety, there may be individuals or subgroups who feel excluded, unsupported, and unsafe. This chapter examines how group identity, inclusion, and exclusion shape psychological safety, with an emphasis on the nuanced experiences of individuals within groups.

PIXAR ANIMATION STUDIOS

Psychological safety is at the heart of creativity and innovation. It creates a space where individuals feel valued, respected, and confident enough to take risks and voice unconventional ideas without fear of embarrassment or retaliation. Pixar Animation Studios has long been celebrated for fostering an environment that exemplifies these principles.[1] Its ability to produce groundbreaking, emotionally resonant films has been linked to the studio's commitment to

DOI: 10.4324/9781003501855-10

trust, inclusion, and openness. Pixar's story is that of embracing diverse perspectives and challenging norms, which has become a key factor in its creative success.

Pixar's films showcase the transformative power of inclusion and trust, often portraying protagonists who struggle with belonging and find strength through connection and collaboration. Here are just a few examples:

- *Inside Out* (2015) explores the vital role of all emotions, including Sadness, and how embracing vulnerability fosters growth.
- *Finding Nemo* (2003). At its core, Finding Nemo is a story about trust. Marlin, a cautious and overprotective father, learns to value Dory's unconventional approach, even when it contrasts sharply with his instincts.
- *The Incredibles* (2004). This film exemplifies how embracing uniqueness leads to collective success. The Parr family's growth as a team only occurs when they accept their individuality.

These films offer emotional, powerful, and enduring lessons about the power of trust and inclusion to foster creativity and collaboration, which also reflects the values Pixar itself strives to embody in its processes as well as its relationships. The studio's "Braintrust" model, where directors and teams receive open, constructive feedback, epitomizes a process embedded in psychological safety. This philosophy has been instrumental in producing some of the most beloved animated films in history, earning Pixar praise for its culture of innovation and respect.[2]

Pixar's commitment to creativity and innovation extended to its hiring practices. When Brad Bird, the director of The Incredibles, joined Pixar, he had just experienced the financial failure of The Iron Giant. Despite his recent setback, Pixar's leaders—Steve Jobs, Ed Catmull, and John Lasseter—invited Bird to "shake things up." Their openness to challenge and experimentation reflected their fear of complacency and their desire to question established ways of thinking.[3]

Bird accepted the challenge and for his first Pixar project, *The Incredibles*, chose what he called "the black sheep"—team members who were frustrated with the status quo and eager to try new approaches. There were huge technical challenges associated with the movie, including animating hair, water, and fire, which this unconventional team overcame. As well as pushing the boundaries of computer animation, the movie was also praised for the psychological depth of its characters to achieve something extraordinary. Bird's willingness to embrace those who "didn't fit in" demonstrated how psychological safety can unlock creativity by empowering marginalized voices.

Pixar's success story seemed to align perfectly with the lessons of its films: trust, inclusion, and respect lead to outstanding results. The studio's openness to experimentation and willingness to take risks cemented its reputation as an exemplar of psychological safety.

Unfortunately, not everyone has the opportunity to experience a working environment like that. Consider this example: A young graphic designer joined a highly respected creative media company, drawn by its reputation for innovation and inclusion. Yet, just two weeks in, she was cornered in the company kitchen by a senior male leader who made inappropriate comments while openly leering at her. Over the next five years, she endured repeated incidents of harassment and exclusion, including being physically groped by a coworker and sidelined from key projects by an informal boys' club system.

In one particularly demoralizing instance, she was uninvited from weekly meetings because the senior leader "had a hard time controlling himself around young women." This exclusion directly affected her ability to contribute to important creative processes and severely limited her career progression. The behavior of the senior leader set a tone for the organization, where other male colleagues felt emboldened to make degrading jokes and dismiss their female peers.

Nor was she the only woman who felt like this. Understanding the risks of openly speaking up, women supported one another informally. Those who challenged inappropriate behavior were labeled "difficult" and faced professional repercussions, including being sidelined or even dismissed. Gender bias was so pervasive that even performance reviews reflected it. The designer was criticized for "designing too many options" and "asking too many questions"—an approach that, as her male mentor later admitted, would have been praised in a man. Physically and emotionally exhausted, she eventually left the company.[4] The company in this distressing case was none other than Pixar.

The very organization celebrated earlier for its groundbreaking creativity and psychological safety was the same place where this young designer, along with other women, experienced exclusion, harassment, and profound psychological insecurity. How could such a stark contrast exist within the same institution? This revelation highlights a critical point: psychological safety is not universal. While some employees may be thriving in an environment that value their contributions, others may face barriers that leave them feeling unsafe, undervalued, and excluded. For all its accolades, there were individuals within Pixar who did not experience the same sense of safety, inclusion, or respect.

THE IMPACT OF EXCLUSION ON PSYCHOLOGICAL SAFETY

The treatment the graphic designer endured would have profoundly undermined her psychological safety. Instead of finding herself in an environment where individuals feel respected, included, and free to contribute without fear of judgment or reprisal, she encountered systemic behaviors that communicated the opposite:

- **Exclusion from Key Opportunities**: Being uninvited from meetings sent a clear signal that her presence and contributions were not valued. This type of exclusion erodes confidence and stifles creativity, leaving individuals disengaged and disempowered.
- **Harassment and Objectification**: The repeated incidents of harassment created a climate of fear and humiliation, making it impossible for her to feel safe or respected. Such behaviors not only violate personal boundaries but also signal that the organization tolerates discrimination.
- **Bias**: Gendered feedback and unequal treatment compounded the designer's sense of alienation. Over time, these messages reinforce the feeling that certain individuals are less capable or deserving.
- **Lack of Accountability**: The organization's failure to address these issues—choosing instead to protect senior leaders—eroded trust, a cornerstone of psychological safety. When individuals see that bad behavior goes unpunished, they are less likely to speak up or take creative risks.

The consequences of such an environment are far-reaching. Employees who feel excluded or unsafe are less likely to innovate, collaborate, or perform at their best. Over time, the organization itself suffers as it fails to harness the full potential of its talent.[5]

Pixar's dual narrative—of groundbreaking creativity and systemic exclusion—offers a powerful lesson. Psychological safety cannot be assumed simply because an organization fosters innovation or produces exceptional results.

This is also a reminder that the work of fostering psychological safety is never complete—it is a continual process of listening, learning, and growing. In my experience, the story that an organization tells about itself can be one of the biggest obstacles that has to be overcome in getting people to accept that bias and prejudice is part of its culture. Pioneering in one way, Pixar was utterly conventional in another.

THE EVOLUTIONARY BASIS OF INCLUSION AND EXCLUSION

Our need to belong is deeply rooted in our evolutionary past.[6] For the longest portion of human evolution, survival depended on belonging to stable groups or tribes. Being ostracized from the group was not just emotionally painful—it was a death sentence. Although our modern environment has shifted dramatically, our psychological wiring remains attuned to subtle signals of inclusion or exclusion.

This evolutionary perspective highlights the significance of small, seemingly inconsequential behaviors in shaping our sense of belonging. For instance, a colleague greeting us warmly as we enter the office, or a leader acknowledging our contribution in a meeting, sends signals that affirm our inclusion in the group. Conversely, being ignored in these situations can trigger feelings of exclusion that undermine psychological safety.

In the context of a team or workplace, the absence of overt conflict does not guarantee psychological safety for everyone. Subtle behaviors, rooted in-group identity and social psychology, can leave some individuals feeling like outsiders, even when the group as a whole is thriving.

SOCIAL IDENTITY THEORY AND ITS RELEVANCE TO PSYCHOLOGICAL SAFETY

Social identity theory (SIT), developed by Henri Tajfel and John Turner,[7] provides a framework for understanding how group membership influences behavior and perceptions. According to SIT, people categorize themselves and others into groups, identify with certain groups, and compare their group to others. This three step process has significant implications for psychological safety:

1. **Categorization**: We simplify our complex social world by categorizing people into groups. While this helps us navigate relationships, it also fosters stereotypes and assumptions, which can undermine psychological safety for individuals who don't fit the dominant group's norms. For example, women in male-dominated workplaces often report being mistaken for support staff or being overlooked in meetings—a subtle but powerful signal that they do not fully belong.

2. **Identification**: Once individuals identify with a group, they derive a sense of self-esteem from their membership. However, this identification can also create in groups and out groups. In workplaces, this manifests in behaviors like favoring team members who share similar backgrounds, interests, or characteristics, while inadvertently sidelining those who are different.

3. **Comparison**: Groups tend to compare themselves to others, often seeking to assert superiority. This tendency can lead to in-group favoritism, where members receive more support, resources, and recognition. For instance, leaders may unconsciously spend more time mentoring in-group members, providing them with critical advantages in career development.

PSYCHOLOGICAL SAFETY FOR THE IN-GROUP VERSUS THE OUT-GROUP

A group may appear psychologically safe when viewed from the perspective of its in-group members. These individuals receive consistent affirmation, feel valued, and experience fewer barriers to expressing themselves. However, out-group members often experience a very different reality. (As a general rule, if someone tells me that there are no out-groups in their organization, they are a part of the in group). The absence of overt hostility does not equate to safety; it is the accumulation of small, everyday behaviors or omissions that signal exclusion.

A useful framework for understanding subtle exclusion is the concept of micro-incivilities. A term you may be more familiar with is microaggressions, which was popularized in the book, Microaggressions in Everyday Life by Derald Wing Sue.[8] I deliberately use this micro-incivilities instead of "microaggressions" because it better aligns with existing organizational theories, such as Thomas Bateman and Dennis Organ's work on organizational citizenship behaviors,[9] which emphasize civility and respectful interactions in workplace settings. By framing these actions as micro-incivilities, we remain grounded in a well-established theoretical model that is highly relevant to professional environments. Furthermore, an aggression cannot be done unknowingly, so when we use the term micro aggression, it automatically eliminates the possibility that someone may have engaged in the behavior unwittingly.

Micro-incivilities are defined as[10] "daily, commonplace behaviors or aspects of an environment that signal, wittingly or unwittingly, to members of out groups that they do not belong and are not welcome." This term acknowledges that individuals may engage in such behaviors without malice or even awareness, which is critical in understanding workplace relationships. Unlike "microaggressions," which can imply intentionality or hostility, micro-incivilities focus on the broader context of organizational behaviors and the unconscious ways exclusion can manifest.

The specific micro-incivilities experienced often depend on one's perceived group membership. For example, women frequently report their ideas being dismissed in meetings, only to be acknowledged when repeated by male colleagues. Others share frustrations about being mistaken for support staff or asked to perform menial tasks like making coffee, subtly reinforcing their perceived lower status in teams. These behaviors, while subtle, can undermine the civility, respect, and inclusion that are central to fostering a psychologically safe workplace. Framing these actions through the lens of organizational citizenship behavior helps clarify their impact and emphasizes the importance of addressing them in a constructive and systemic way.

Micro-Incivility in Action

Imagine a weekly team meeting where the leader regularly praises certain team members for their contributions but overlooks others. Over time, the excluded individuals may internalize a sense of unworthiness or irrelevance, even if the omissions were unintentional. Similarly, the leader might unconsciously make more eye contact with in-group members, fostering a subtle but significant divide. These behaviors may seem trivial to those who are not on the receiving end, but for the out-group members, they erode psychological safety.

The Hidden Costs of Exclusion

The impact of exclusion on psychological safety is profound. Research highlights four key mechanisms through which exclusion affects individuals:[11]

1. **Physiological Stress**: Exclusion triggers the release of cortisol, the stress hormone, which impairs decision-making and cognitive performance. For instance, an employee who feels excluded might struggle to focus during critical tasks, reducing their effectiveness and increasing their anxiety.
2. **Self-Monitoring**: Individuals who have experienced exclusion often become hyper-aware of their environment, scanning for further signs of rejection. This heightened vigilance diverts mental energy from productive work, contributing to a cycle of diminished performance and increased alienation.
3. **Task-Related Worries**: Excluded individuals may second-guess their actions, fearing judgment or criticism. A team member hesitant to share their ideas in meetings, for example, may miss opportunities to contribute and grow.

4. **Suppression of Thoughts**: Attempts to suppress feelings of exclusion place an additional cognitive burden on individuals, further impairing their ability to perform complex tasks.

These mechanisms not only undermine individual performance but also have ripple effects on team cohesion and organizational outcomes. When individuals feel excluded, they are less likely to seek support or collaborate with colleagues, further isolating themselves and limiting the team's overall effectiveness.

NETWORKS AND THE DYNAMICS OF INCLUSION

Informal networks play a critical role in shaping psychological safety. Social network analysis reveals that the most powerful networks in organizations often exclude individuals who differ from the majority. Factors like homophily (the tendency to associate with similar others), density (the strength of connections within a network), and multiplexity (overlapping social and professional ties)[12] create barriers for out-group members.

In a law firm, a network analysis conducted by myself and colleagues revealed a dense inner circle dominated by male leaders, with women disproportionately represented in the outer group. The inner circle had greater access to information, opportunities, and influence, perpetuating gendered dynamics of exclusion. While the firm as a whole prided itself on being inclusive, the reality for many women was a lack of psychological safety and limited career prospects.

THE ROLE OF LEADERS IN FOSTERING INCLUSION

Leaders have a pivotal role in shaping the psychological safety of their teams. By recognizing the impact of micro-incivilities and actively working to include out-group members, leaders can create a more equitable environment. Simple actions—like ensuring

Identity Threat Cues

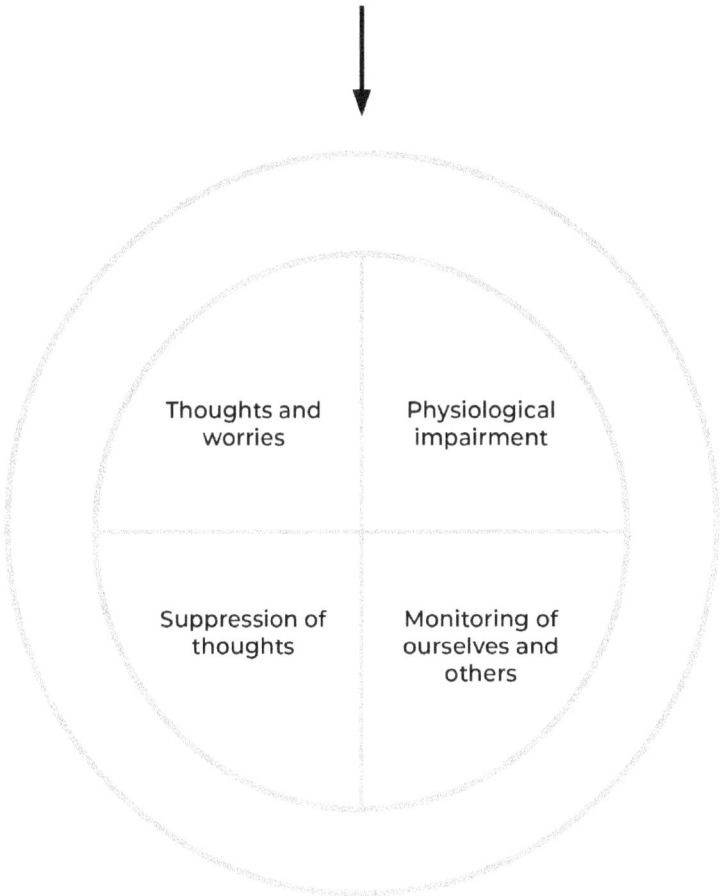

Figure 8.1 Impact of Identity Threat Cues on Performance

everyone's ideas are heard in meetings or acknowledging the contributions of all team members—can have a significant impact.

A senior HR leader recounted an incident where she joined a conversation among male colleagues discussing football. Despite her genuine interest and knowledge of the sport, the conversation shifted to rugby and then to cricket, each time excluding her participation. This subtle exclusion highlighted how in-group dynamics can marginalize others, even when no overt hostility is present. For the HR leader, the experience reinforced the need for deliberate efforts to foster inclusivity in workplace interactions.

PSYCHOLOGICAL SAFETY FOR MARGINALIZED GROUPS

Visual differences such as gender[13] and ethnicity[14] can be used to exclude. Other groups face unique challenges in achieving psychological safety, particularly when their identities are not immediately visible. LGBTQ+ individuals, for example, may hesitate to come out at work due to fears of stigma or exclusion. Microincivilities like heteronormative assumptions can compound this sense of alienation.

Similarly, individuals with disabilities often encounter the "spread phenomenon,"[15] where their disability influences others' perceptions of their overall competence. For instance, a wheelchair user might be praised excessively for completing routine tasks, reinforcing stereotypes of inadequacy.

While fostering psychological safety at the group level is important, it is equally critical to address the experiences of individuals and subgroups. Leaders must move beyond surface-level assessments of team dynamics and delve into the nuanced realities of inclusion and exclusion.

There are actions that leaders can take, including:

- **Recognizing Biases**: Acknowledge the potential for in-group favoritism and actively seek to engage out-group members.

- **Encouraging Diverse Networks**: Promote cross-functional collaboration and mentorship opportunities to break down silos.
- **Addressing Micro-Incivilities**: Provide training on unconscious bias and create channels for employees to share their experiences.
- **Monitoring Inclusion**: Use tools like social network analysis to identify patterns of exclusion and address them proactively.

CONCLUSION: PSYCHOLOGICALLY SAFE FOR WHO?

Psychological safety is not a binary state; it exists on a spectrum and can vary widely within the same group. A team may appear cohesive and high-performing, yet some members may feel isolated and unsupported. By asking "Psychologically safe, but for who?," organizations can move beyond superficial assessments and take meaningful steps to ensure that every individual feels included, valued, and safe.

This deeper understanding of psychological safety requires acknowledging the subtle dynamics of in-groups and out-groups, the impact of exclusion on individuals, and the role of leaders in fostering truly inclusive environments. When organizations embrace these complexities, they can unlock the full potential of their teams, ensuring that psychological safety is not just a privilege for some but a reality for all.

CASE STUDY: ANTISEMITISM—THE IMPACT OF EXTERNAL TRIGGER EVENTS ON PSYCHOLOGICAL SAFETY

The intersection of external geopolitical events and workplace dynamics can profoundly affect employees' psychological safety, engagement, and overall sense of inclusion. When events occur outside of the organization, they can serve as a spur for some people to display prejudice and hostility toward a specific targeted group.

These events are known as trigger events, and research has revealed how these have

> galvanised bigoted sentiment towards an out group. For a minority, in the aftermath of these trigger events, their prejudices become bolstered to such an extent that for a temporary period they cannot contain them within their minds. They felt the need to evacuate them with violent force onto those perceived to be associated with the event.[16]

On October 7, 2023, a series of coordinated attacks were launched by Hamas militants on multiple locations in southern Israel, marking one of the deadliest days in the region's recent history. Over a thousand lives were lost, including men, women, children, and elderly individuals, while hundreds were taken hostage and transported into Gaza.

The attacks shocked the world due to their scale, brutality, and the deliberate targeting of civilians. Survivors recounted harrowing accounts of violence, including massacres at music festivals and residential areas. In response, Israel declared a state of war, initiating large-scale military operations in Gaza aimed at dismantling Hamas's infrastructure and rescuing the hostages.

The events of October 7 and the subsequent escalation of the Israel–Gaza conflict sent shockwaves globally, reigniting tensions and deeply polarizing societies. For Jewish communities worldwide, the attacks were profoundly traumatic, compounding fears of rising antisemitism and bringing historical and cultural anxieties to the fore. These developments underscored the fragility of psychological safety for Jewish individuals in workplaces and public spaces as political and social discourse intensified. This case study describes research we at Pearn Kandola carried on antisemitism in the UK following the events of October 7, 2023 and subsequently the findings highlight the necessity for organizations to address these challenges proactively to foster a supportive and inclusive environment.

This study included a survey, a focus group and a series of interviews conducted with Jewish employees.

KEY FINDINGS FROM THE SURVEY

The survey data highlighted concerning trends in the experiences of Jewish employees regarding religious discrimination and inclusion.

Comfort with Sharing Religious Identity

- Only 58% of Jewish employees felt comfortable sharing their religion with colleagues, and this number dropped slightly when considering new colleagues (55%) and clients (54%).
- In contrast, 43% of Jewish respondents admitted to hiding their religious practices at work to avoid negative comments or stereotyping.

One respondent stated, "I don't wear my Star of David at work anymore. It's upsetting, but safety is the priority."

Experiences of Discrimination

- 39% of Jewish respondents reported directly experiencing religious discrimination in the workplace, and 66% said they had either experienced or witnessed it.
- 34% reported verbal harassment, and 20% indicated they had faced physical harassment at work, underscoring the severity of the issue.

One participant explained, "I've been told, 'You don't look Jewish' or 'You don't act Jewish.' How am I supposed to respond to that? It's dehumanizing."

Micro-Incivilities

- A staggering 80% of Jewish employees reported experiencing micro-incivilities in the workplace, with many stating these incidents occur regularly.
- Comments such as "You people run the media" or "You killed Jesus" were cited as common examples.

A participant reflected the behaviors "aren't always overt, but they wear you down over time. It makes you feel like you don't belong."

Emotional Impact

The survey revealed profound emotional consequences for Jewish employees in the workplace:

- 29% reported feeling hurt, 28% felt angry, and 28% felt scared.
- The fear of expressing one's identity was common, with one respondent noting, "It feels like we're living in the 1930s. Antisemitism isn't muted anymore; it's out in the open, and it's terrifying."

INSIGHTS FROM INTERVIEWS: FIRST-PERSON ACCOUNTS

The interviews provided a deeper understanding of how antisemitism affects psychological safety for Jewish employees. Participants shared their lived experiences, emphasizing the detrimental impact on their well-being and workplace engagement.

Fear and Safety Concerns

Fear emerged as a dominant theme. Many respondents described feeling unsafe due to the rise in antisemitic incidents, both in public and at work.

- One interviewee shared, "I live on the fringes of Golders Green, and there's been a lot of police presence. A grocery store near me was attacked. It's made me nervous even going to the shops."
- Another explained the anxiety caused by public protests: "The protests in London have been terrifying. People shout 'Free Palestine,' but the undertone is clearly antisemitic. It's not safe to display anything Jewish."

In workplaces, fear often manifested as self-censorship. One respondent revealed, "I don't talk about my faith or where I go on weekends. I won't wear anything that shows I'm Jewish. It's just not worth the risk."

Experiences of Exclusion

Exclusion and isolation were recurring themes. Many Jewish employees reported feeling unsupported by their organizations, especially in the wake of October 7th.

- One participant recounted, "During Black Lives Matter, everyone was reaching out to Black colleagues to show support. After October 7th, there was silence for Jewish employees. It was like our pain didn't matter."
- Another shared, "I asked my line manager why leadership didn't send a note of support after October 7th, and he said, 'We don't comment on these things.' It felt like a betrayal."

Even when support was offered, it was often seen as insufficient. One respondent noted, "The email said antisemitism and Islamophobia wouldn't be tolerated. But they didn't ask people to reach out to Jewish colleagues. It felt hollow."

Emotional and Psychological Toll

The emotional toll of antisemitism was deeply felt by participants. Many described a pervasive sense of fear, anxiety, and exhaustion.

- One interviewee stated, "I have a two-year-old son, and I'm scared for him. What kind of world is he going to grow up in?"
- Another reflected on the cumulative effect of micro-incivilities: "It's the small comments, the jokes about Jews and money, that build up over time. It makes you question your place in the workplace."

The trauma of recent events was particularly acute. One respondent said, "After October 7th, I couldn't focus at work. I kept refreshing the news and reading about the massacres. I asked to work from home because I just couldn't face people."

ORGANIZATIONAL RESPONSES: SUCCESSES AND SHORTCOMINGS

What Organizations Did Well

It's always instructive to look at what has been done well, and some organizations took meaningful steps to support Jewish employees, which were deeply appreciated:

- **Proactive Communication**: One respondent praised their employer for sending a supportive message after October 7th: "The email acknowledged the pain Jewish employees might be feeling and encouraged us to reach out to leadership if we needed help. It was a small gesture, but it meant a lot."
- **Recognition of Jewish Holidays**: Some companies were commended for acknowledging Jewish holidays. A participant noted, "The senior partner sends messages on Jewish holidays. It shows that we are seen and valued."

- **Encouraging Allyship**: One participant highlighted a positive example: "Our sales director asked us to reach out to Israeli colleagues and be supportive. It made a difference knowing someone cared."

What Organizations Could Have Done Better

However, many respondents felt their organizations failed to address antisemitism effectively:

- **Lack of Visible Support**: Several participants expressed disappointment at the absence of organizational statements condemning antisemitism. One noted, "During other crises, like Ukraine, there was an outpouring of support. But when it's about Jewish people, there's silence."
- **Failure to Educate Employees**: Many respondents emphasized the need for education around antisemitism. One explained, "People don't understand the nuances of being Jewish. They conflate Judaism, Israel, and Zionism. Organizations need to educate their staff to combat ignorance."
- **Inconsistent Responses to Discrimination**: A recurring complaint was the inconsistent handling of antisemitic incidents. One participant shared, "If someone made a racist comment about another group, there would be consequences. But with antisemitism, it's brushed under the rug."

PSYCHOLOGICAL SAFETY: A CRITICAL CONCERN

The lack of psychological safety for Jewish employees was a pervasive issue. Psychological safety was deeply compromised for many respondents.

Impact on Identity

Many Jewish employees felt they had to suppress their identity to fit in:

- "I'm proud to be Jewish, but I've stopped sharing that part of myself at work. It's too risky."
- "People don't know I'm Jewish, and that's how I like it. I don't want to draw attention to myself in this environment."

Impact on Engagement and Performance

The fear of discrimination and exclusion significantly impacted employees' ability to engage fully at work:

- "I'm constantly second-guessing what I say and do. It's exhausting."
- "I've stopped contributing in meetings because I don't feel safe. What if someone makes a comment that I can't respond to?"

Impact on Retention

Several participants considered leaving their jobs due to a lack of support:

- "I left my last job because they refused to accommodate my Jewish holidays. It was clear they didn't value me."
- "I'm actively looking for a new role. I don't want to stay in an organization that doesn't support its Jewish employees."

RECOMMENDATIONS FOR ORGANIZATIONS

To foster psychological safety and inclusivity for Jewish employees, organizations must take the following steps:

1. **Proactively Address Antisemitism**: Issue clear, visible statements condemning antisemitism, particularly during periods of heightened tension.
2. **Educate Employees**: Implement training programs to increase awareness of antisemitism and Jewish identity.
3. **Create Safe Spaces**: Establish forums where Jewish employees can share their experiences and concerns without fear of judgment.
4. **Ensure Consistent Responses**: Develop clear policies for addressing antisemitic incidents, with consistent consequences for offenders.
5. **Recognize Jewish Identity**: Acknowledge Jewish holidays and accommodate religious practices to show support and inclusivity.

CONCLUSION

The experiences shared by Jewish employees highlights how a trigger event impacted Jewish employees in organizations and how this left them feeling psychologically unsafe. It shows how global events, which may not impact many people in organizations thousands of miles away, may have some people within them, who have been profoundly affected.

Organizations and all of us who work in them can be better informed about trigger events and then take proactive steps to support targeted colleagues. In doing so organizations can create environments where all employees feel valued and secure, ultimately fostering greater engagement and productivity. Without such efforts, the fear and exclusion faced by, in this case, Jewish employees will continue to undermine their well-being and professional contributions.

CASE STUDY: JACINDA ARDERN AND THE POWER OF INCLUSIVE LEADERSHIP IN BUILDING PSYCHOLOGICAL SAFETY

Jacinda Ardern, the former Prime Minister of New Zealand, is widely recognized for her empathetic leadership and progressive policies. Known for her ability to connect with diverse communities, Ardern has become a global symbol of compassion, inclusivity, and decisive action in the face of challenges.[17]

Her leadership style is a combination of analytical skills and a notable ability to balance pragmatism with empathy. Her approach to engaging with communities who may feel marginalized, particularly the Māori and Muslim populations, demonstrated her ability to build trust, foster psychological safety, and lead with compassion in the face of adversity.

BUILDING RELATIONSHIPS WITH THE MĀORI COMMUNITY

Ardern's commitment to improving relationships with the Māori community went beyond rhetoric. Her actions symbolized a significant shift in the government's approach to engaging with indigenous groups. Historically, Waitangi Day, a national day marking the signing of the Treaty of Waitangi, had often been a site of political tension. In 2018, Ardern broke with tradition by spending five days at Waitangi, instead of the cursory one-day visits typical of past leaders.

She emphasized listening to the grievances of the community and committed to tangible actions. For the first time, a female prime minister was granted speaking rights at Te Whare Rūnanga, the meeting house on Treaty Grounds. In her speech, she invited the community to hold her government accountable, saying,

> Ask us what we have done to give dignity back to your whānau [family], ask us what we have done to improve poverty for tamariki [children], ask us what we have done to give

rangatahi [Young people] opportunities and jobs. Ask us, hold us to account.

Ardern's approach extended to symbolic gestures that conveyed respect and partnership. She instructed her team to forgo a traditional catered breakfast in favor of a public barbecue, where she and her ministers cooked for the attendees. This act of service reinforced her message that the government was there to work collaboratively with the Māori community.

A Māori commentator noted the transformative nature of her engagement, saying, "Such a different vibe this Waitangi. It's almost like all you need to do is listen and be respectful of historical grievances for people to feel reassured." This reflected a broader impact: by listening and taking concrete steps, Ardern fostered a sense of psychological safety, allowing marginalized voices to feel heard and respected.

RESPONDING TO SEXUAL HARASSMENT WITHIN HER PARTY

Ardern's response to sexual harassment allegations within the Labour Party showed her willingness to address systemic issues directly, even at the cost of potential political fallout. Allegations of sexual harassment and assault by a party staffer revealed failings in how complaints were handled. Young female members reported feeling dismissed and unsupported, which uncovered an attitude of neglect within the party.

Ardern's response was swift and unequivocal. She publicly apologized on behalf of the Labour Party, stating, "We have a duty of care, and we failed in it." Rejecting excuses or minimizing the issue, she appointed a Queen's Counsel to conduct an independent review of the complaints and introduced measures to overhaul the party's complaint-handling processes. These included implementing sexual harassment training and creating a volunteer code of conduct.

In contrast to Pixar, where sexual harassment claims had been downplayed or ignored for years before change was implemented, Ardern demonstrated a proactive and transparent approach. Her actions reassured not only the complainants but also the broader public that accountability and change were non-negotiable. By taking ownership of the issue, she sent a powerful message about the importance of psychological safety and trust.

SUPPORTING THE MUSLIM COMMUNITY AFTER THE CHRISTCHURCH MASSACRE

The Christchurch mosque shootings, on March 15, 2019, were among the darkest moments in New Zealand's history, claiming the lives of 51 people. Ardern's response to the tragedy highlighted her ability to lead with compassion, inclusiveness, and decisiveness.

Within hours of the attack, Ardern addressed the nation, unequivocally condemning the violence as terrorism and affirming the victims' place in New Zealand. "Many of those who will have been directly affected by this shooting may be migrants to New Zealand. They have chosen to make New Zealand their home, and it is their home. They are us," she said.

In the days following the attack, Ardern visited grieving families and the wider Muslim community, wearing a hijab as a mark of respect. Her gesture resonated deeply within the community, with one mourner later saying, "She didn't just come to show support; she embraced us in our grief." Photographs of Ardern embracing Muslim women became a global symbol of solidarity, with one image even being projected onto the Burj Khalifa in Dubai alongside the Arabic word for peace, "Salam."

Ardern's leadership extended beyond symbolic acts. She committed to addressing the underlying issues that enabled the attack, including gun law reforms to ban semi-automatic weapons. She also called on social media platforms to take greater responsibility for preventing the spread of hate speech.

The Muslim community noted her genuine support, including ensuring financial aid for affected families regardless of immigration status and facilitating the burial process for victims. Her actions created a sense of psychological safety, reassuring the community that their government was committed to protecting their rights and well-being.

KEY TAKEAWAYS FOR ORGANIZATIONS

1. **Listening and Respect**: Ardern's engagement with the Māori community demonstrates the power of listening and respecting historical grievances. Organizations can learn from this by creating spaces where marginalized voices feel heard and valued.
2. **Transparency and Accountability**: Ardern's handling of sexual harassment allegations highlights the importance of addressing systemic issues with transparency and urgency. Organizations must establish robust systems for handling complaints and ensure accountability at every level.
3. **Empathy in Leadership**: Ardern's response to the Christchurch tragedy underscores the importance of empathetic leadership in times of crisis. By standing with affected communities and taking tangible actions, leaders can foster trust and unity.
4. **Proactive Change**: Ardern's approach to gun law reforms and party culture shifts illustrates the need for proactive measures. Organizations should not wait for crises to act but should continually assess and improve their systems to prevent harm.

Jacinda Ardern's leadership provides a blueprint for building meaningful connections with communities and fostering psychological safety within organizations. Her ability to combine compassion with decisive action ensures that all voices are included, respected, and supported.

KEY POINTS

Psychological safety, inclusion, and organizational norms are all inextricably linked. highlighting the importance of deliberate actions to create truly inclusive workplaces. What this chapter has demonstrated is that psychological safety for some doesn't mean that it exists for all. Some groups can feel marginalized and their experiences ignored even within environments celebrated for innovation or inclusion.

The case studies examined in this chapter—Pixar and Jacinda Ardern's leadership—offer powerful lessons in both the successes and failings of fostering psychological safety. Pixar had an exalted reputation for creativity and openness-for some of its people. It was the same organization that failed to protect women employees from harassment and exclusion. This serves as an important reminder that psychological safety requires consistent effort across all levels of an organization. Whilst it was pioneering and pushing the boundaries in its productions, it was at the same time deeply old-fashioned in its attitudes toward women. Ensuring every employee feels valued, respected, and safe demands more than broad cultural values—it necessitates accountability, robust policies, and actions that address the blatant and the subtle ways people can be excluded.

In contrast, Jacinda Ardern's leadership provides a blueprint for fostering inclusion and psychological safety on a national scale.

Her commitment to listening, transparency, and empathy enabled her to address grievances effectively and build trust with marginalized communities, such as the Māori and Muslim populations. Her approach after the Christchurch massacre demonstrated the power of empathetic leadership, combining symbolic gestures with decisive actions like gun law reforms and financial support for victims. Ardern's leadership style highlights the importance of addressing exclusion head-on, respecting diverse identities, and creating space for collaboration.

The chapter also explores the mechanisms through which exclusion undermines psychological safety. Micro-incivilities, such as being overlooked in meetings or facing subtle biases, can erode individuals' confidence and engagement. Trigger events, such as external crises or conflicts, further amplify these challenges, as seen in the experiences of Jewish employees after the October 7, 2023, attacks.

For organizations, these issues present a call to action: address bias proactively, educate employees, and foster an environment where all voices are heard and valued.

Ultimately, the work of fostering psychological safety and inclusion is never finished. It is a continuous process that requires leaders and organizations to listen, learn, and adapt.

GLOSSARY

Social Identity Theory. A theory by Henri Tajfel and John Turner explaining how group membership shapes behavior. SIT involves:

1. Categorization: Classifying people into groups, which can foster stereotypes and undermine inclusion.
2. Identification: Aligning with a group for self-esteem, often creating in-groups and out-groups.
3. Comparison: Groups compare to others, leading to favoritism and unequal opportunities.

SIT reveals how group dynamics impact psychological safety and inclusion in workplaces.

In-groups and out-groups. In social identity theory, in-groups are the groups individuals identify with and feel a sense of belonging to, while out-groups are those they perceive as different or outside their group. In-groups often receive more support, trust, and opportunities, whereas out-groups may face exclusion or unequal treatment, impacting inclusion and psychological safety.

Micro-incivilities. "Daily, commonplace behaviors or aspects of an environment that signal, wittingly or unwittingly, to members of out-groups that they do not belong and are not welcome." This term acknowledges that individuals may engage in such behaviors without malice or even awareness, which is critical in understanding workplace relationships. Unlike "microaggressions," which can imply intentionality or hostility, micro-incivilities focus on the broader context of organizational behaviors and the unconscious ways exclusion can manifest.

Networks. Informal networks significantly influence psychological safety within organizations. Social network analysis (SNA) is a tool to understand these dynamics, revealing how powerful networks often exclude individuals who differ from the majority. Factors such as homophily (associating with similar others), density (strength of network connections), and multiplexity (overlapping social and professional ties) can create barriers for out-group members, limiting their inclusion and opportunities.

Trigger events. Trigger events are external geopolitical or societal incidents that significantly impact workplace dynamics, particularly psychological safety and inclusion. These events can provoke prejudice and hostility toward specific groups, and highlight the need for organizations to acknowledge and address these to maintain a safe and inclusive environment.

NOTES

1 Amy Edmondson (2018). *The Fearless Organization: Creating Psychological Safety in the Workplace for Learning, Innovation, and Growth.* Wiley.
2 Catmull, E. & Wallace, A. (2014). *Creativity, Inc.: Overcoming the Unseen Forces That Stand in the Way of True Inspiration.* Bantam.
3 Rao, H., Sutton, R. & Webb, A.P. (2008). Innovation lessons from Pixar: An interview with Oscar-winning director Brad Bird. *McKinsey Quarterly, 4*(1), pp. 1–9.

4 https://variety.com/2018/film/news/pixar-boys-club-john-lasseter-cassandra-smolcic-1202858982/

5 Clark, Timothy R. (2020). *The 4 Stages of Psychological Safety: Defining the Path to Inclusion and Innovation*. Berrett-Koehler Publishers.

6 Giphart, R. & Van Vugt, M. (2018). *Mismatch: How our Stone Age Brain Deceives Us Every Day (and What We Can Do About It)*, Robinson

7 Tajfel, H. & Turner, J.C. (1979). An integrative theory of inter-group conflict. In Austin, W. & Worschel, S., eds. *The Social Psychology of Intergroup Relations*. Brooks/Cole Publishing Company

8 Sue, D.W. (2009). *Microaggressions in Everyday Life: Race, Gender and Sexual Orientation*. Wiley.

9 Bateman, T.S. & Organ, D.W. (1983). Job satisfaction and the good soldier: the relationship between affect and employee "citizenship." *Academy of Management Journal*, *26*(4), pp. 587–595

10 Kandola, B. (2018). *Racism at Work: The Danger of Indifference*. Pearn Kandola Publishing, p. 101

11 Taylor, J. (2020). *How Discrimination Affects Our Performance in Free to Soar: Race and .Well-being in Organisations* Pearn Kandola Publishing.

12 Lazarsfeld, P.F. & Merton, R.K. (1954). Friendship as a social process: a substantive and methodological analysis, in Berger, M. ed., *Freedom and Control in Modern Society*, Van Nostrand, pp. 18–66

13 Ibarra, H. (1992). Homophily and differential returns: Sex differences in network structure and access in an advertising firm. *Administrative Science Quarterly*, 37(3), pp. 422–447.

14 Mehra, A., Kilduff, M., & Brass, D.J. (1998). At the margins: a distinctiveness approach to the social identity and social networks of underrepresented groups. *Academy of Management Journal*, *41*(4), pp. 441–452

15 Wright, B. (1963). *Physical Disability: A .Psychological Approach* Harper & Row, p. 118

16 Williams, M. (2022). *The Science of Hate: How Prejudice Becomes Hate and What We Can Do to Stop It.* Faber and Faber, p. 125

17 Chapman, M. (2020). *Jacinda Ardern: A New Kind of Leader*. Auckland: Allen & Unwin.

FURTHER READING

Chapman, M., 2020. Jacinda Ardern: A New Kind of Leader. Auckland: Allen & Unwin.

Clark, Timothy R., 2020. *The 4 stages of psychological safety: Defining the path to inclusion and innovation.* Berrett-Koehler Publishers.

Kandola, B., 2018. *Racism at work: The danger of indifference.* Pearn Kandola Publishing.

Tajfel, H. and Turner, J.C., 1979. An integrative theory of intergroup conflict. In Austin, W.G. and Worchel, S. eds., *The social psychology of intergroup relations.* Monterey, CA: Brooks/Cole.

PART III
THE SYSTEMIC VIEW

Culture, structure, and the hidden forces that shape safety at scale.

This part uses socio-technical systems theory to explore how organizational culture, structure, and processes interact to support or undermine psychological safety—offering a framework to analyze and change the system, not just individual behavior.

DOI: 10.4324/9781003501855-11

9

HOW CAN I USE THE IDEAS IN THIS BOOK TO CARRY OUT AN ANALYSIS OF PSYCHOLOGICAL SAFETY IN MY ORGANIZATION?

INTRODUCTION

The focus on psychological safety within teams and the actions we can take to develop it are undeniably important and valuable. Teams are the essential units where much of the collaborative work takes place, and psychological safety can significantly enhance performance, creativity, and engagement. However, this is not the whole picture. If we were to focus exclusively on teams, we would risk overlooking critical organizational factors that impact the team but exist outside of its immediate boundaries.

It is essential to broaden our perspective and consider how organizational culture, systems, and structures enable or hinder psychological safety.

The issues and ethical failings related to Lance Armstrong and the drug-taking in cycling were not only due to the behavior of powerful individuals and their impact on the teams. It was the complicity of the governing body, the International Cycling Union (UCI), that undoubtedly reinforced the cheating. David Walsh highlighted how the UCI failed to enforce anti-doping regulations by actively prioritizing the sport's commercial interests.[1]

DOI: 10.4324/9781003501855-12

By shielding high-profile riders like Armstrong from scrutiny, the UCI sent a clear message: success was more important than integrity. This institutional authority validated the doping culture, making it appear as though the behavior was sanctioned at the highest levels. Riders who might have resisted doping were discouraged by the knowledge that the governing body itself was complicit in maintaining the system—and, apart from the media, who else could they complain to.

In this chapter, I want to bring all the things we have covered in the book together to be able to conduct an organizational analysis, which can provide an overview of the factors that enable or detract from psychological safety.

ENABLERS OF PSYCHOLOGICAL SAFETY

It is understood and widely accepted that psychological safety plays a critical role in open communication and mitigating risks in teams. Remaining at this level of analysis, however, means that we may miss broader organizational forces at play that are having a strong influence on the interactions between team members.

High stakes environments, such as healthcare and aviation, feature prominently in the psychological safety literature. This is understandable as the decisions that people make are genuinely a matter of life and death. People can act, or fail to act, in ways that seem incomprehensible with hindsight and which can lead to tragic outcomes not just for others but for themselves too. It's all too easy to see events like this as the result of relationships between the people directly involved, and if we were satisfied with this, we may fail to see the other forces that are influencing the behavior and attitudes of the team members.

Recent research provides complementary and valuable insights into how safety voice and safety listening operate within teams, with implications that extend beyond high stakes environments into other organizational settings.

In a task that could not have been easy, researchers carried out a detailed analysis of cockpit voice recorder (CVR) transcripts from 172 aviation accidents.[2] The results challenge the assumption that accidents primarily stem from a lack of safety voice. Instead, their findings revealed that safety voice—the act of raising concerns about hazards—was nearly always present before accidents occurred. However, these concerns were frequently ignored or dismissed, leading to communication breakdowns that contributed to accidents. This demonstrates that while psychological safety encourages individuals to speak up, its impact is limited if safety listening—the acknowledgment of and acting on concerns—is lacking.

Other research[3] found that muted safety voice and safety silence often stemmed from respect for hierarchy and from first officers (FOs) feeling undervalued or disrespected by captains. Where captains micromanaged FOs or subjected them to sexist or racist comments, they created a climate where psychological safety was undermined, reducing the likelihood of safety voice. Issues of psychological safety are clearly manifested in team behaviors, but they are also possibly reflective of broader organizational culture.

Recommendations for improving psychological safety and open communication include captains soliciting input, using inclusive language, admitting their own fallibility, and creating a sense of team unity. Captains who engage with their crew on an equal footing—emphasizing collaboration over hierarchy—are more likely to encourage safety voice. For instance, phrases like "We are a crew. None of us is infallible, so feel free to question anything" help establish a culture where team members feel valued and empowered to raise concerns.

These findings also highlight that psychological safety is not solely about encouraging individuals to speak up but also about creating recognition that organizational, and indeed national, cultures must also be addressed. Organizations must go beyond the team analysis to embedding psychological safety into their cultures, which means looking at other areas including policies, processes and workflows.

As well as aviation, literature reviews of psychological safety in a wide range of sectors, including healthcare,[4] sport,[5] and hospitality[6] have identified organizational culture factors as enablers of psychological safety as well as team dynamics.

From this research we can see consistent cross-sector themes relating to organizational factors including:

- Clarity of roles and expectations: Employees know who to report to and what is expected in their roles.
- Commitment to continuous improvement, including frequent feedback sessions, open forums, and performance reviews aimed at growth rather than blame.
- Support for diversity and inclusion: such as inclusive policies for hiring and training on how to respect differences.
- Onboarding processes that emphasize the organization's commitment to psychological safety.
- Leaders visibly addressing harmful behaviors, such as bullying or exclusion, and creating a culture of accountability.
- Clear reporting systems-employees know where and how to report safety concerns or interpersonal conflicts without fear of retaliation.

Training programs are not just functional but also enable collaboration and inclusion such as:

- Regular workshops or simulations that improve both technical and interpersonal skills.
- Growth opportunities: Employees supported to develop their skills through mentorship, constructive feedback, and fair performance evaluations.
- Leadership development programs where aspiring leaders learn how to develop psychological safety in their teams.

ARE INDUSTRY-SPECIFIC TRAITS TRULY DIFFERENT?

It's interesting to note that whilst these themes cut across the sectors, the focus and the language used may well be different. While industry-specific traits may have different emphases, such as risk management in aviation or emotional healing in sports, these reflect contextual nuances of the same principle—having organizations that engender trust through psychological safety.

Analysis of the industry-specific traits reveals that they are less about unique practices and more about contextual priorities. For instance:

- Risk management in aviation reflects the high stakes of safety failures but also mirrors healthcare's focus on patient outcomes or sports' emphasis on physical and emotional safety.
- Emotional healing in sports may seem distinct but parallels hospitality's focus on managing stress and burnout.
- The "just culture" in aviation is a formalized system, yet its essence fits with the psychological safety principles of fairness and non-retaliation seen across all sectors.

Thus, these are not different approaches but variations tailored to meet the specific operational, emotional, and social demands of each sector. Industry-specific adaptations, such as error reporting systems in aviation or stress management programs in hospitality, align with the shared goal of ensuring employees feel physically and psychologically safe. By aligning the exploration of psychological safety with the sector's challenges, terminology, and values, we can ensure the concept resonates more with employees and stakeholders, leading to meaningful organizational change.

BUT HOW DO WE CARRY OUT AN ORGANIZATIONAL ANALYSIS?

Deep underground, in the confined and dimly lit tunnels of a British coal mine, the introduction of new coal-cutting machinery was causing unexpected challenges. Teams that had once worked well together, relying on each other for safety and efficiency, found their relationships strained. The new technology, introduced to increase productivity, disrupted established ways of working and redefined roles, creating confusion and tension among workers. Tasks that were once shared harmoniously now became sources of disagreement, and the sense of trust and collaboration that had characterized these teams began to erode. When researchers from the Tavistock Institute were brought in to investigate, they uncovered a crucial insight: technological advancements, no matter how promising, cannot be implemented in isolation. The social and organizational contexts in which these changes occur are equally critical.

This realization became the foundation of socio-technical systems (STS) thinking—a framework that has since provided a profound understanding of the interdependence between social and technical systems and their role in shaping organizational success. Edgar Schein, who along with Warren Bennis coined the term "psychological safety," was an expert and advocate of STS.[7]

Building on this work, socio-technical systems theory evolved as a framework to optimize the interplay between social and technical components within organizations. Early applications of STS thinking focused on heavy industry, later extending to advanced manufacturing, office-based environments, and information technology. Over the decades, researchers at Leeds University Business School under the expert guidance of Professor Chris Clegg and colleagues have refined and expanded the approach, culminating in the development of the socio-technical systems hexagon.[8]

This model represents organizational systems as a set of six interdependent elements—people, tasks, structure, technology, goals, and infrastructure—embedded within a broader external environment. By visualizing these relationships, the hexagon offers a practical and systematic way to analyze, understand, and improve complex organizational systems.

The methodology recognizes that changes in one part of a system—whether technological, structural, or social—inevitably ripple through other components, necessitating a holistic perspective. Key principles underpinning this approach include:

1. **Systemic Design**: Viewing organizations as interconnected systems that require simultaneous optimization of social and technical factors.
2. **Stakeholder Engagement**: Involving diverse stakeholders—end-users, managers, designers, and external experts—in the design process to capture multiple perspectives and ensure buy-in.
3. **Iterative Feedback**: Using an iterative process of data collection, analysis, and stakeholder feedback to refine findings and recommendations.
4. **Evaluation and Adaptation**: Continuously evaluating the system's performance and adjusting to align with changing goals and circumstances.

This methodology is applied through a combination of qualitative and quantitative techniques, including interviews, surveys, process mapping, and systems modeling. It emphasizes the importance of multidisciplinary collaboration and iterative refinement to ensure robust outcomes.

The Leeds University Business School team have used the STS hexagon in a wide variety of contexts including crowd disasters, failures in leadership and infrastructure design.[9] Disasters often stem from a combination of fragmented coordination, inadequate training, and insufficient stakeholder engagement—failures that could have been mitigated through better socio-technical design.

Socio-Technical Systems and Psychological Safety

STS can be used to assess psychological safety at different points and levels within an organization. By examining how people interact with technology, structures, and processes, the framework can pinpoint areas where employees feel unsupported, misunderstood, or disempowered.

By applying STS thinking, organizations can move beyond reactive problem-solving to a more proactive stance. As well as analyzing past failures the methodology's ability to map interdependencies and simulate different scenarios allows it to predict where problems may arise. For instance, it can identify bottlenecks in task allocation, misalignments between goals and infrastructure, or risks stemming from insufficient training.

SIX DIMENSIONS FOR THE SOCIO-TECHNICAL SYSTEMS MODEL OF PSYCHOLOGICAL SAFETY

I have adapted to six dimensions to help analyze psychological safety in organizations. Three of the scales—leader, team and inclusion–were presented earlier in the book. They are now supplemented by three further scales—goals, policies, and structure.

Each of the six scales highlights a key dimension of psychological safety, collectively addressing the behaviors, policies, structures, and systems that contribute to a safe and inclusive work environment. The scales can be used by you to look at an organizational perspective on psychological safety. You can also use the checklist for any specific aspects that you are interested in. I would encourage you to use this with teams as well as to identify organizational enhancers and obstacles to psychological safety.

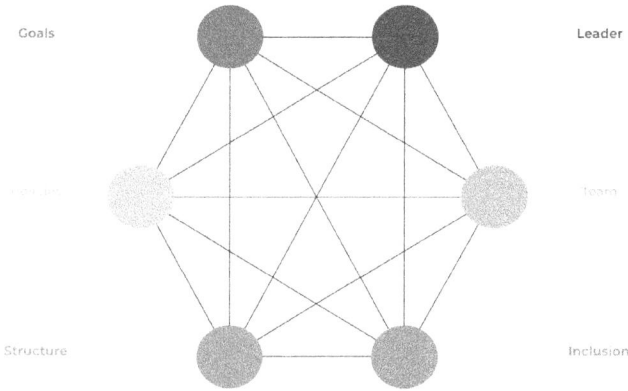

Figure 9.1 Socio-Technical Systems Model to Analyze Psychological Safety in Organizations

1. Leader: Observational Checklist for Leader

The Leader dimension evaluates the practices of leaders in enabling psychological safety by modeling trust, fairness, and inclusivity.

1. The leader actively encourages all team members to share their opinions, regardless of rank or seniority.
2. Team members feel comfortable challenging the leader's ideas without fear of retribution.
3. The leader demonstrates empathy by addressing the individual challenges faced by team members.
4. Feedback from the leader is constructive, focusing on improvement rather than blame.
5. The leader openly admits their own mistakes and demonstrates vulnerability.
6. The leader mediates conflicts fairly, ensuring all parties feel heard and respected.
7. Meetings led by the leader are structured to ensure that all voices, including quieter members, are heard.

8. The leader frames mistakes and failures as learning opportunities rather than as reasons for criticism.
9. Decisions made by the leader are transparent, with the rationale clearly communicated to the team.
10. The leader invests time in coaching and developing the skills of their team members.

2. Team: Observational Checklist for Team

The Team dimension assesses the level of psychological safety within teams, emphasizing collaboration, trust, and openness among team members.

1. Team members feel comfortable sharing concerns and ideas without fear of retaliation or judgment.
2. Meetings are structured to ensure that all team members have the opportunity to contribute.
3. Alternative viewpoints and constructive dissent are recognized and valued during team discussions.
4. Mistakes are openly discussed and reframed as opportunities for team learning and growth.
5. Team members acknowledge and appreciate one another's contributions regularly.
6. Feedback within the team is constructive and focused on improvement rather than assigning blame.
7. Team members trust one another to act in the best interest of the team.
8. The team regularly participates in retrospectives or debriefs to improve processes and communication.
9. Team members support one another during challenges and actively collaborate to find solutions.
10. Successes are celebrated as collective achievements rather than focusing solely on individual contributions.

3. Inclusion: Observational Checklist for Inclusion

The Inclusion dimension measures the organization's commitment to creating an inclusive environment where all employees feel psychologically safe, regardless of identity, role, or status.

1. Inclusion initiatives are visibly supported by leadership and address the needs of all employees, including contractors and part-time staff.
2. Employees across all roles and identities feel safe expressing their ideas and concerns without fear of retaliation.
3. Policies and practices ensure equitable treatment across different roles, departments, and geographical locations.
4. The organization actively supports marginalized identities and traditionally undervalued roles through mentorship, recruitment pipelines, or other programs.
5. Teams consistently practice allyship, addressing challenges faced by internal and external collaborators.
6. Workspaces (physical and virtual) are designed to be accessible, inclusive, and welcoming to all.
7. Structural designs promote collaboration across departments and minimize organizational silos.
8. Cross-team collaboration ensures that employees, regardless of job function or contract status, contribute to decisions.
9. Secure systems allow all employees to report harassment, discrimination, or bullying without fear of reprisal.
10. Leaders are held accountable for inclusivity efforts, with transparent updates on progress and challenges.

4. Goals Scale: Observational Checklist for Goals

The Goals dimension examines the alignment of organizational objectives and performance targets with psychological safety and employee well-being.

1. Goals are clearly communicated across all levels of the organization.
2. Goals emphasize both performance outcomes and employee well-being.
3. Employees understand how their individual and team objectives align with organizational goals.
4. Performance expectations are realistic and achievable without creating undue pressure.
5. Ethical considerations are integrated into goal-setting processes.
6. Employees feel involved in setting or refining team and individual goals.
7. Short-term goals are balanced with long-term objectives to prevent burnout or excessive pressure.
8. Organizational priorities are consistent and not frequently changing without clear rationale.
9. Employees feel supported with adequate resources to achieve their goals.
10. Leadership regularly reviews and adapts goals based on feedback and changing circumstances.

5. Policies: Observational Checklist for Policies

The Policies dimension assesses the impact of organizational policies—such as performance management, hiring, anti-harassment, and grievance procedures—on psychological safety

1. The organization's performance management system prioritizes growth and learning over punitive measures.
2. Policies explicitly discourage ranking systems that create unhealthy competition (e.g., "rank-and-yank" approaches).
3. Anti-harassment policies are well-communicated and strictly enforced.
4. Employees feel comfortable reporting harassment, discrimination, or bullying without fear of retaliation.

5. Hiring policies emphasize effectiveness with fairness in all stages of recruitment.
6. Policies actively promote fair treatment and equal opportunities for all employees.
7. Performance reviews include consideration of teamwork, collaboration, and psychological safety contributions.
8. Clear procedures exist to address grievances, and they are consistently followed.
9. Training on harassment, unconscious bias, and inclusivity is mandatory and regularly updated.
10. Employees perceive HR and management as supportive in addressing policy-related concerns.

6. Structure: Observational Checklist for Structure

The Structure dimension evaluates how organizational hierarchies, reporting lines, and decision-making processes impact psychological safety.

1. Reporting lines are clear, and employees know who to approach for guidance and support.
2. Organizational hierarchies allow open communication across all levels.
3. Leadership accessibility is encouraged through formal and informal mechanisms (e.g., open-door policies).
4. Employees feel empowered to share ideas, regardless of their rank or position.
5. Cross-departmental collaboration is encouraged and facilitated by the organizational structure.
6. Decision-making processes are transparent, with input sought from relevant stakeholders.
7. Organizational structures minimize silos and encourage knowledge-sharing.

8. Employees understand how their roles fit into the broader organizational structure.
9. Mechanisms are in place to resolve conflicts or role ambiguities effectively.
10. The organizational structure adapts to support evolving team and individual needs.

To see the checklists in use I have applied them to two case studies: Boeing and General Motors.

CASE STUDY: THE CHANGING DNA OF BOEING—FROM ENGINEERS TO SHAREHOLDERS[10]

It was 73 seconds into its flight, on January 28, 1986, when the Space Shuttle Challenger broke apart killing all seven of its crew members. President Reagan immediately established a commission to discover why this disaster had occurred. One member of the commission said that such a collapse of oversight and accountability would never have occurred in his organization.

This verdict was delivered by Joe Sutter, the legendary engineer who led the development of the 747, and the company he worked for was Boeing. The aircraft manufacturer was one of the most respected and revered organizations, not just in America, but in the world with an unsurpassed reputation for its uncompromising stance on safety. Yet, as events unfolded, it became evident that the company he held in high regard would descend into a culture of cost-cutting, regulatory complacency, and silenced voices—a toxic blend that proved catastrophic.

The seeds of Boeing's downfall were planted in the 1990s during a corporate transformation following its merger with McDonnell Douglas. Historically, Boeing was an engineering-driven company that valued innovation and quality above all else. Engineers were empowered to voice concerns, and the culture embraced the philosophy that "bad news is welcome," ensuring potential risks were addressed before products reached the market. This ethos was evident in programs like the 777, where rigorous testing and collaboration were at the heart of its success.

However, the merger brought a seismic shift. Leaders like Harry Stonecipher, a disciple of General Electric's Jack Welch, introduced a shareholder-focused model that prioritized financial metrics over technical excellence. Cost-cutting became the mantra, sidelining engineers in favor of executives more skilled at reading balance sheets than aeronautical details. Boeing transformed from an engineering powerhouse into what some called a "shareholder-friendly creature of the market."

A RACE AGAINST TIME: THE 737 MAX

The 737 MAX program crystallized the cultural and systemic flaws that had emerged. Pressured by competition from Airbus's fuel-efficient A320neo, Boeing opted to retrofit the aging 737 platform rather than design a new aircraft. This decision was driven by cost and speed, not engineering considerations.

Integrating larger engines onto the 737 altered its aerodynamics, shifting the plane's center of gravity. To compensate, Boeing introduced the Maneuvering Characteristics Augmentation System (MCAS), software designed to prevent stalls. To save costs, Boeing ensured the MAX would not require additional pilot training. As a result, MCAS was downplayed in pilot manuals and poorly understood by those who would rely on it in emergencies.

THE DECLINE OF PSYCHOLOGICAL SAFETY

One of the most damaging shifts at Boeing was the erosion of psychological safety—the ability of employees to voice concerns without fear of retaliation. Historically, engineers were encouraged to raise issues and propose solutions. However, under the shareholder-driven model, this culture of openness was systematically dismantled. Engineers who flagged risks, like those associated with the MAX, were ignored or even punished.

Engineers who questioned design compromises that prioritized cost and schedule over safety, were dismissed and constant layoffs created a pervasive sense of anxiety.

This environment suppressed dissent and prioritized meeting deadlines over addressing risks. Managers dismissed warnings, and the culture of "go/no-go meetings" descended into "go/go meetings," where dissent was simply not an option.

REGULATORY COMPLACENCY: THE FAA AND BOEING'S COZY RELATIONSHIP

Adding to the crisis was a troubling shift in regulatory oversight. Over the years, the Federal Aviation Administration (FAA) had ceded much of its authority to Boeing, effectively allowing the company to self-certify aspects of its aircraft. One FAA insider described the agency as acting "in service of Boeing, not to police them."

When Boeing submitted its safety assessment for MCAS, the FAA reviewed an outdated version of the software, unaware of key changes, such as MCAS's increased authority to repeatedly force the plane's nose down. This lack of scrutiny allowed critical flaws to persist, setting the stage for disaster.

THE CRASHES: TRAGEDY EXPOSED

On October 29, 2018, Lion Air Flight 610 plunged into the Java Sea minutes after takeoff. Less than five months later, on March 10, 2019, Ethiopian Airlines Flight 302 suffered a similar fate. In both cases, MCAS activated repeatedly due to faulty sensors, overpowering pilots' attempts to regain control.

These crashes exposed the dangers of Boeing's cost-cutting and lack of transparency. Pilots were unaware of MCAS's behavior because it was barely documented in manuals. The engineers who could have foreseen these issues had been silenced by a culture that valued profits over safety.

A CULTURE OF DENIAL AND DEFLECTION

In the aftermath of the crashes, Boeing's response further eroded public trust. The company initially blamed, with more than a hint of racism, pilot error, deflecting attention from its internal failings. Internal emails later revealed a cavalier attitude toward safety, with one pilot describing the MAX as "designed by clowns, who in turn are supervised by monkeys."

CEO Dennis Muilenburg assured the public of the MAX's safety, even as internal data estimated the risk of 15 additional crashes without a software fix. Despite mounting evidence of design flaws, Boeing resisted grounding the fleet, prioritizing shareholder confidence over passenger safety.

ASSESSING PSYCHOLOGICAL SAFETY AT BOEING

To understand the role of psychological safety in Boeing's failings, each indicator was scored out of five and then reached an overall rating on each of the six dimensions using the Red, Amber, Green system, each highlighting a different facet of the company's dysfunctions.

1. Leadership (Red)

Leadership at Boeing was characterized by suppression of dissent and a lack of empathy. Employees who raised safety concerns were punished or dismissed. Leaders prioritized cost and deadlines over transparency, and mistakes were punished rather than treated as learning opportunities. For example, a manager remarked, "People have to die before Boeing will change things." This leadership style created a culture of fear, stifling the open communication necessary for psychological safety and innovation.

2. Teams (Red)

Teams at Boeing operated under immense pressure, with engineers and staff fearful of raising concerns. Collaboration was hampered by layoffs and outsourcing, which fragmented institutional knowledge. Retrospectives and team debriefs were often skipped, leaving systemic risks unaddressed. This lack of trust and collaboration led to critical safety oversights, such as the unchecked design and implementation of MCAS.

3. Inclusion (Red)

Boeing's inclusivity efforts were superficial at best. Contractors, particularly those overseas or on visas, were undervalued and underpaid. These disparities created a two-tiered workforce, marginalizing certain roles and voices. Cross-departmental collaboration was rare, further isolating employees and limiting diverse perspectives. Leadership failed to champion collaboration and inclusivity, exacerbating the disconnect between teams and individuals. Moving the headquarters to Chicago from Seattle was done explicitly to reduce the influence of engineers, which sent clear signals to the organization about who and what was valued.

4. Goals (Amber)

Boeing's goals were clear and well-communicated, but they were misaligned with psychological safety principles. The company's race to compete with Airbus's A320neo prioritized cost and schedule over safety and employee well-being. However, some elements of goal-setting were functional. Employees understood organizational priorities, and leadership maintained consistent timelines. Yet this clarity often came at the expense of undue pressure, forcing employees to make compromises that jeopardized safety.

5. Policies (Red)

Boeing's policies, such as the "rank-and-yank" performance system, fostered unhealthy competition and eroded teamwork. Anti-harassment and grievance mechanisms were inconsistently enforced, leaving employees reluctant to report misconduct. While some policies aimed to promote accountability, their uneven implementation undermined trust and transparency, contributing to the toxic culture.

6. Structure (Amber)

Boeing's structure was a mix of legacy stability and post-merger dysfunction. Reporting lines were generally clear, and employees understood their roles. However, structural silos and fragmented decision-making hindered collaboration and knowledge-sharing.

For instance, engineers designing MCAS were in a different division from the test pilots evaluating it, leading to critical communication gaps. Despite these weaknesses, some elements of the structure retained functionality, hence the Amber rating.

Table 9.1 *Summary of Scores and Ratings*

Dimension	*RAG Rating*	*Key Insights*
Leadership	**Red**	Suppressed dissent, punished mistakes, prioritized profits over safety.
Teams	**Red**	Lack of trust and collaboration led to critical safety oversights.
Inclusion	**Red**	Marginalized groups and weak cross-departmental collaboration.
Goals	**Amber**	Clear but misaligned with safety and well-being priorities.
Policies	**Red**	Inconsistent enforcement fostered a toxic and inequitable culture.
Structure	**Amber**	Fragmented collaboration but retained some legacy stability.

CONCLUSION: A HOUSE DIVIDED

The 737 MAX crisis exposed the depths of Boeing's failings, particularly in leadership, team dynamics, and policies. While some areas, like goals and structure, retained elements of functionality, the broader cultural and organizational dysfunctions overshadowed these strengths.

This case serves as a stark reminder that psychological safety is essential—not optional. Boeing is urgently trying to rebuild trust within its workforce and prioritize safety to prevent future tragedies. Restoring its reputation will depend on its ability to align its goals with both engineering excellence and employee well-being. Will it be possible? The next case study shows how it can be done.

CASE STUDY: TRANSFORMING GENERAL MOTORS—MARY BARRA'S JOURNEY TO A CULTURE OF ACCOUNTABILITY AND SAFETY

In December 2013, Mary Barra shattered the glass ceiling as she ascended to the role of CEO at General Motors (GM), becoming the first woman to lead a major global automaker. Her promotion marked a historic milestone, but she faced skepticism both within and outside the company. Critics dismissed her appointment as a symbolic gesture, a diversity hire designed to soften GM's image in the wake of its bankruptcy and bailout. However, Barra would soon prove these assumptions wrong as she confronted one of the company's gravest crises—the ignition switch defect scandal.

A HISTORY OF COMPLACENCY AND CULTURAL SILOS

Before Barra's tenure as CEO, GM had long had a fragmented, siloed culture. Departments functioned in isolation, with little communication or collaboration. This culture enabled systemic failures, such as the decade-long delay in recalling vehicles equipped with a faulty ignition switch.

The defect, linked to at least 45 fatalities, became a glaring symbol of GM's prioritization of cost-cutting over customer safety. A critical internal report highlighted that while numerous employees had identified the issue, no one took responsibility to address it. This "history of failures," as the report described, was emblematic of a corporate culture that shunned accountability.

Barra, a GM veteran who had risen through the ranks from the factory floor, inherited a company with deeply entrenched practices. GM's legacy was one of producing "crappy cars," as Barra herself bluntly stated, and of failing to prioritize the consumer experience. The challenges ahead demanded not only operational improvements but also a profound cultural transformation.

CONFRONTING CRISIS WITH TRANSPARENCY AND ACCOUNTABILITY

The ignition switch scandal erupted just months into Barra's tenure as CEO. Under immense scrutiny from Congress, regulators, and the public, Barra faced the daunting task of addressing the crisis while restoring trust in GM. Her approach to the scandal exemplified a leader committed to fostering a culture of accountability and psychological safety.

Barra met with the families of victims, offering personal apologies and expressing genuine remorse. Her actions contrasted sharply with GM's historical tendency to deflect blame. Barra ordered a comprehensive review of all pending recalls, ultimately recalling a staggering 32 million vehicles within a year. Recognizing the systemic issues that had allowed the defect to persist, she launched the "Speak Up for Safety" initiative, encouraging employees at all levels to report safety concerns without fear of retribution. This program marked a pivotal step toward dismantling the culture of fear that had stifled transparency and accountability at GM.

A LEADER FOCUSED ON COMMUNICATION AND INCLUSION

Barra's leadership philosophy was rooted in clear communication, rational clear thinking and inclusivity. Drawing on lessons from her early career in manufacturing and engineering, she emphasized the importance of engaging employees at every level.

During the bankruptcy period, Barra introduced systems to ensure workers understood how their roles contributed to broader business outcomes. She applied an engineering mindset to communications, implementing standardized scorecards and metrics that aligned plant performance with corporate goals. These measures not only improved operational efficiency but also fostered a sense of shared purpose.

As CEO, Barra continued to prioritize communication. She held town halls, "brown bag" lunches, and meetings with employees across the organization, creating platforms for open dialogue. Her approach reflected her belief that empowering employees to voice their ideas and concerns was essential for driving innovation and preventing future crises.

Barra also championed initiatives to promote diversity and inclusion within GM. Recognizing that culture change required institutional support, she established employee resource groups and expanded recruitment efforts to historically underrepresented communities, such as Howard University. By addressing barriers to inclusion, Barra sought to build a workforce that reflected GM's diverse customer base.

TRANSFORMING GM'S CULTURE AND OPERATIONS

Barra's cultural reforms extended to GM's operational practices. Under her leadership, the company adopted a consumer-first approach, encapsulated in her no-nonsense four-word mandate: "No more crappy cars." She streamlined decision-making processes, reducing bureaucracy and holding individuals accountable for their contributions. For instance, she consolidated the oversight of each car model under a single executive, eliminating the inefficiencies of having multiple leaders with conflicting priorities.

Barra's insistence on quality over cost also marked a departure from GM's past practices. While mindful of budget constraints, she prioritized investments that directly enhanced the customer experience, such as safety features and design improvements. Her ability to bridge the gap between finance and engineering helped align GM's goals with its mission of delivering reliable, high-quality vehicles.

PSYCHOLOGICAL SAFETY AS A CATALYST FOR CHANGE

At the heart of Barra's turnaround strategy was her commitment to fostering psychological safety—a work environment where employees felt safe to voice concerns and take risks without fear of blame. Barra understood that the absence of psychological safety had been a root cause of GM's failures, enabling a culture of complacency and silence. By creating channels for open communication and embedding accountability into GM's processes, Barra began to rebuild trust within the organization. Her leadership demonstrated that psychological safety was not a soft skill but a critical driver of innovation, quality, and resilience.

THE ROAD AHEAD

Mary Barra's transformation of GM is a testament to the power of leadership grounded in accountability, transparency, and empathy. Her leadership has returned GM to profitability with 2024 expected to be the company's best year in its history.

Her ability to confront crisis head-on, while addressing deep-seated cultural issues, positioned GM for a future defined by excellence rather than mediocrity. Barra's leadership offers a blueprint for creating a psychologically safe and inclusive workplace—one where employees are empowered to speak up, take ownership, and contribute to a shared vision of success.

This analysis is the same that was carried out in the earlier case study and highlights how Barra's leadership transformed GM's culture and operational practices, with a focus on psychological safety as the cornerstone of her turnaround strategy.

1. Leader (Green)

Barra consistently demonstrated strong leadership practices aligned with psychological safety. She encouraged open communication, as seen by her direct engagement with employees during brown bag lunches and her establishment of the "Speak Up for Safety" initiative. Barra displayed empathy through her interactions with victims' families and her efforts to reinstate a worker nearing retirement. She also provided constructive feedback, framing challenges as opportunities for improvement.

2. Team (Amber)

While Barra fostered collaboration, particularly by breaking down silos between manufacturing and product engineering teams, the organization initially struggled with open communication and trust. GM's legacy of silos inhibited teamwork, but Barra's efforts, such as cross-functional attendance in team meetings and the use of scorecards, began to address these issues. However, the long-standing cultural fragmentation meant there was room for improvement in psychological safety at the team level.

3. Inclusion (Green)

Barra implemented numerous initiatives to improve inclusion at GM, such as expanding recruitment to Historically Black Colleges and Universities (HBCUs) and creating employee resource groups. Her emphasis on diversity and inclusion extended beyond symbolic gestures; she actively worked to build an environment where underrepresented voices were heard. Additionally, her leadership style, which valued input from union workers and employees across hierarchies, supported an inclusive culture.

4. Goals (Green)

Barra clearly articulated GM's objectives, such as her famous "No more crappy cars" directive, which aligned quality and customer satisfaction with organizational priorities. She emphasized long-term goals, such as quality improvements, over short-term fixes. Her restructuring efforts, including holding individuals accountable for specific vehicle models, created realistic and achievable performance expectations. However, the legacy of GM's pre-bankruptcy misaligned goals, which prioritized cost-cutting at the expense of quality, presented challenges she had to overcome.

5. Policies (Amber)

Barra's tenure included significant improvements in policies that promoted safety and accountability. The "Speak Up for Safety" program encouraged employees to report concerns without fear of retaliation. Barra also streamlined policies to focus on clear and actionable outcomes, such as her simplification of the company's dress code. However, GM's history of failing to enforce safety standards, as revealed by the ignition switch scandal, underscored the need for more consistent policy application.

6. Structure (Amber)

Barra implemented structural reforms that reduced silos and improved communication, such as integrating manufacturing and product development teams and assigning clear accountability for vehicle models. However, GM's legacy of fragmented hierarchies and poor cross-departmental collaboration meant that structural barriers to psychological safety were deeply ingrained. Her introduction of the SPQRCE (Safety, People, Quality, Responsiveness, Cost, Environment) metrics system and focus on transparency marked significant progress, but cultural inertia slowed the pace of change.

OVERALL ANALYSIS

Mary Barra's leadership at GM marked a critical shift toward psychological safety, emphasizing inclusion, transparency, and accountability. While her reforms significantly improved GM's organizational culture, the legacy of organizational silos and poor safety practices highlighted the need for continued transformation. The RAG assessment reflects a journey in progress, with Green ratings in leadership, inclusion, and goals, and Amber ratings in team dynamics, policies, and structure, signaling areas for further development.

Table 9.2 *Summary of Ratings and RAG Assessment*

Dimension	RAG Rating	Description
Leader	Green	Barra fostered trust, empathy, and transparency, though early crisis handling could improve.
Team	Amber	Progress in collaboration was evident, but silos and historical mistrust persisted.
Inclusion	Green	Significant progress in diversity initiatives and valuing diverse perspectives.
Goals	Green	Aligned goals with safety and quality, but legacy misalignments created challenges.
Policies	Amber	Positive reforms like "Speak Up for Safety," though historical inconsistencies remained.
Structure	Amber	Structural reforms improved collaboration, but silos remained a barrier.

KEY POINTS AND CONCLUSION

In this book, I have sought to explain what psychological safety is, its benefits, and applications. Much of the work on psychological safety has been very fruitfully applied to teams within organizations. Whilst valuable, I feel that this prevents us from looking at other factors which may foster or frustrate the development of psychological safety in our organizations. I have looked at the role of leaders, teams, and each one of us in ensuring that we each play our part in making our working environments safe for everyone. Socio-technical systems theory, however, demonstrates that by focusing on people, that's only half of the system that we need to understand.

So, in this chapter, I have looked at organizational goals, policies, and structure. By applying this approach, with the checklists provided, we are able to analyze organizations in terms of their culture and the strengths they have in terms of psychological safety and the risks that may also exist. By analyses like this, we are able to build on the strengths and mitigate some of the weaknesses. Ultimately, this approach equips organizations with the tools to create resilient, adaptive systems that not only achieve their goals but also support the well-being of their people.

PSYCHOLOGICAL SAFETY: THE OVERLOOKED KEY TO ORGANIZATIONAL SUCCESS?

As we close this exploration into psychological safety, it's important to reflect on its journey from relative obscurity to its present state—a concept that is simultaneously better recognized yet often misunderstood.

In the introduction, I discussed the stark reality: even in rooms filled with seasoned executives, the term "psychological safety" is met with blank stares. Only recently I met a very experienced and respected psychology professor at a UK business school taunting the audience to admit to "believing" in psychological safety, as if it was some sort of cult. His challenging, if not condescending, questioning of the attendees was met with not a single person responding. He had predictably, and highly ironically, demonstrated the existence of psychological safety by his very behavior.

This limited recognition becomes even more troubling when contrasted with the aftermath of high-profile organizational failures. Whether in the corporate boardroom, a governmental agency, or a high-stakes engineering project, the post-mortem analyses are often replete with mentions of technical errors, process breakdowns, or lapses in regulatory compliance.

Rarely, however, do these investigations probe into the cultures of silence, fear, and suppressed voices that enabled those failures. Even in inquiries led by public bodies or governmental commissions, the absence of psychological safety is a glaring yet unexamined factor. The Chilcot Inquiry into the Iraq War, had identified the very characteristics of the lack of psychological safety (dominant, charismatic leadership; groupthink; ignoring dissenting voices) yet made no recommendations about how governments and cabinets should conduct themselves to ensure that they do not fall into the same trap again. It is no surprise, therefore to find that a recent analysis of UK governments cabinets has shown that little has changed. On the other hand, why should it have changed because no recommendations addressed this topic.

Nor is it only in the United Kingdom. In 2023, Neil Chenoweth and Edmund Tadros of the *Australian Financial Review* provided an in-depth examination of the PwC (Price Waterhouse Coopers) tax scandal, revealing how the firm exploited confidential government information for commercial gain.[11] The investigation centered on Peter Collins, PwC Australia's former head of international tax, who, between 2014 and 2017, participated in confidential government consultations aimed at curbing multinational tax avoidance. Collins signed multiple confidentiality agreements during this period. However, he breached these agreements by sharing sensitive information with at least 53 PwC partners and staff, both domestically and internationally. This breach enabled PwC to develop strategies that allowed multinational clients, including tech giants like Google and Facebook, to circumvent impending tax laws, thereby undermining the government's efforts to enhance tax compliance.

The article highlighted PwC's initial attempts to downplay the breach as the actions of a single rogue partner. However, internal communications revealed a broader complicity within the firm, with numerous partners aware of and involved in leveraging the confidential information for client advantage. This systemic issue pointed to significant ethical lapses and a culture prioritizing profit over integrity.

The exposé also detailed the regulatory response, including investigations by the Australian Taxation Office and the Tax Practitioners Board, which led to Collins' suspension and intensified scrutiny of PwC's practices. The scandal prompted calls for greater accountability and transparency within the consulting industry, emphasizing the need for robust ethical standards to prevent such breaches in the future. The Australian government announced a package of reforms in August 2024 focused on regulatory measures, for example, whistleblower protection, and stricter penalties for misconduct. PwC initiated its own internal reforms, including the appointment of non-executive directors and a bolstering of oversight powers.

However, the issues of decision-making and psychological safety, the inability call out unethical behavior, and the defensiveness when caught were not addressed at all.

At the same time as this scandal is occurring they have one that has blown up in China and they have been fined a record amount by the UK financial regulator. Is this a systemic issue within this giant organization? Well, you will have to ask PwC about that one.

At first glance, you might think that the decision to go to war in the Middle East by the UK Government would share nothing in common with the decisions made by accountants on the other side of the world. And yet fundamentally the decision-making processes were the same and underneath it all was a lack of psychological safety.

Consider the cultural undercurrents in some of the most devastating corporate and public crises. When employees feel unable to raise concerns—whether about safety, ethics, or operational inefficiencies—organizations lose the opportunity to address issues before they snowball into disaster. Leaders who fail to model openness and vulnerability unwittingly create environments where problems fester in the shadows, shielded by fear of retribution or embarrassment. These patterns are not aberrations; they are symptoms of a deeper systemic neglect of psychological safety.

Yet, even as the term itself gains traction, there is a danger that psychological safety becomes more of a catchphrase than a meaningful practice. Leaders may invoke it in team-building exercises or mission statements without truly understanding the responsibility it entails. Worse, it can devolve into a platitude—emptily referenced without the structural and cultural changes needed to make it a lived reality. This shallow adoption undermines its transformative potential and risks reducing it to yet another business fad.

The real tragedy, however, lies in the missed opportunities. When policymakers or investigative bodies neglect to examine the psychological environment of failed organizations, they fail to address one of the root causes of those failures. Structural reforms, regulatory updates, and even new leadership cannot compensate for a culture where employees feel unsafe to speak up. Without acknowledging this, organizations are doomed to repeat the same mistakes under new banners.

It would be encouraging to think that psychological safety is becoming more recognized in both theory and practice. But recognition is not enough. If it remains a misunderstood buzzword—invoked but not implemented—it risks becoming a hollow promise. For psychological safety to truly drive progress, it must be embedded into the fabric of organizations, championed by leaders who understand its nuances and supported by systems that reward openness and learning.

The challenge moving forward is clear: to move psychological safety from the periphery of leadership thinking to the center of organizational strategy. Only then can we hope to create workplaces that not only achieve extraordinary results but do so sustainably, ethically, and humanely. In the end, the cost of ignoring psychological safety is too high—for businesses, for individuals, and for society as a whole.

GLOSSARY

Socio-technical systems (STS) theory. A framework first developed from research by the Tavistock Institute, which revealed the importance of aligning technological changes with social and organizational contexts. STS was later refined and expanded by Professor Chris Clegg and his team at Leeds University Business School, who developed the socio-technical systems hexagon to systematically analyze and improve complex organizational systems across industries. It emphasizes the interdependence of six key elements: people, tasks, structure, technology, goals, and infrastructure, within a broader environment.

NOTES

1 Walsh, D. (2013). *Seven Deadly Sins: My Pursuit of Lance Armstrong.* Simon & Schuster.

2 Noort, M.C., Reader, T.W., & Gillespie, A. (2021). Safety voice and safety listening during aviation accidents: Cockpit voice recordings reveal that speaking-up to power is not enough. *Safety Science, 139*, pp. 105260–105274. https://doi.org/10.1016/j.ssci.2021.105260

3 Perkins, K., Ghosh, S., Vera, J., Aragon, C. & Hyland, A. (2022). The persistence of safety silence: How flight deck microcultures influence

the efficacy of crew resource management. *International Journal of Aviation, Aeronautics, and Aerospace*, *9*(3), p. 6.

4 O'Donovan, R. & Mcauliffe, E. (2020). A systematic review of factors that enable psychological safety in healthcare teams. *International Journal for Quality in Health Care*, *32*(4), pp. 240–250.

5 Vella, S.A., Mayland, E., Schweickle, M.J., Sutcliffe, J.T., McEwan, D., & Swann, C. (2024). Psychological safety in sport: A systematic review and concept analysis. *International Review of Sport and Exercise Psychology*, *17*(1), pp. 516–539.

6 Vakira, E., Shereni, N.C., Ncube, C.M. and Ndlovu, N. (2023). The effect of inclusive leadership on employee engagement, mediated by psychological safety in the hospitality industry. *African Journal of Hospitality, Tourism and Leisure*, 12(2), pp. 484–500.

7 Schein, E.H. with Schein, P. (2017). *Organisational Culture and Leadership* (5th edition). Wiley.

8 Clegg, C.W., Robinson, M.A., Davis, M.C., Bolton, L.E., Pieniazek, R.L., & McKay, A. (2017). Applying organizational psychology as a design science: A method for predicting malfunctions in socio-technical systems (PreMiSTS). *Design Science*, *3*, p. e6.

9 Clegg, C.W., Robinson, M.A., Davis, M.C., Bolton, L.E., Pieniazek, R.L., & McKay, A. (2017). Applying organizational psychology as a design science: A method for predicting malfunctions in socio-technical systems (PreMiSTS). *Design Science*, *3*, p. e6.

10 Robison. P. (2021) *Flying Blind: The 737 MAX Tragedy, and the Fall of Boeing.* Penguin Business.

11 Chenoweth, N. & Tadros, E. (2023). The inside story of PwC's tax scandal. *Australian Financial Review*, pp. 6–7.

FURTHER READING

Clegg, C.W., Robinson, M.A., Davis, M.C., Bolton, L.E., Pieniazek, R.L. and McKay, A., 2017. Applying organizational psychology as a design science: A method for predicting malfunctions in socio-technical systems. *Design Science*, 3, p. 6.

Robison, P., 2021. *Flying blind: The 737 MAX tragedy and the fall of boeing.* Doubleday.

Vlasic, B., 2014. *Once upon a car: The fall and resurrection of America's big three automakers.* William Morrow.

BIBLIOGRAPHY

Abrams, D. and Levine, J.M., 2012. The formation of social norms: Revisiting Sherif's autokinetic illusion study. In: S. Hogg and J.M. Levine, eds. Social Psychology: Revisiting the Classic Studies. London: SAGE, pp. 57–75. Available at: https://www.researchgate.net/publication/314120328_The _formation_of_social_norms_Revisiting_Sherif's_autokinetic_illusion_ study [Accessed 10 July 2025].

Ahmad, I. and Umrani, W.A., 2019. The impact of ethical leadership style on job satisfaction: Mediating role of perception of Green HRM and psychological safety. Leadership & Organization Development Journal, 40(5), pp. 534–547.

Alhasnawi, H.H. and Abbas, A.A., 2021. Narcissistic leadership and workplace deviance: A moderated mediation model of organizational aggression and workplace hostility. Organizacija, 54(4), pp. 334–349.

American Psychiatric Association, 2013. Diagnostic and statistical manual of mental disorders. 5th ed. Arlington, VA: American Psychiatric Association.

Andersson, M., Moen, O. and Brett, P.O., 2020. The organizational climate for psychological safety: Associations with SMEs' innovation capabilities and innovation performance. Journal of Engineering and Technology Management, 55, p. 101554.

Appelbaum, Nital P. PhD, Santen, Sally A. MD, PhD, Perera, Robert A. PhD, Rothstein, William MD, Hylton, Jordan B. DO and Hemphill, Robin R. MD, MPH, 2022. Influence of psychological safety and organizational support on the impact of humiliation on trainee well-being. Journal of Patient Safety, 18(4), pp. 370–375, June. | DOI: 10.1097/ PTS.0000000000000927

Asch, S.E., 1955. Opinions and social pressure. Scientific American, 193(5), pp. 31–35.

Babiak, P. and Hare, R.D., 2006. *Snakes in suits: When psychopaths go to work*. Regan Books/Harper Collins Publishers.

Baer, M. and Frese, M., 2003. Innovation is not enough: Climates for initiative and psychological safety, process innovations, and firm performance. *Journal of Organizational Behavior*, 24(1), pp. 45–68.

Baguio, C.A. and Heggem, E., 2021. *What strengthens and weakens psychological safety in sales teams under Covid-19 and sudden virtuality?* (Master's thesis), Handelshøyskolen BI.

Bandura, A., 1986. Social Foundations of Thought and Action: A Social Cognitive Theory. Englewood Cliffs, NJ: Prentice-Hall, pp. 23–28.

Bartels, J.M. and Griggs, R.A., 2019. Using new revelations about the Stanford prison experiment to address APA undergraduate psychology major learning outcomes. *Scholarship of Teaching and Learning in Psychology*, 5(4), p. 298.

Bateman, T.S. and Organ, D.W., 1983. Job satisfaction and the good soldier: The relationship between affect and employee 'citizenship'. *Academy of Management Journal*, 26(4), 587–595.

Bean, C., Harlow, M., Mosher, A., Fraser-Thomas, J. and Forneris, T., 2018. Assessing differences in athlete-reported outcomes between high and low-quality youth sport programs. *Journal of Applied Sport Psychology*, 30(4), pp. 456–472.

Binyamin, G., Friedman, A. and Carmeli, A., 2018. Reciprocal care in hierarchical exchange: Implications for psychological safety and innovative behaviors at work. Psychology of Aesthetics, Creativity, and the Arts, 12(1), pp. 104–114. https://doi.org/10.1037/aca0000102

Blomqvist, K. and Cook, K.S., 2018. Swift trust: State of the art and future research directions. In Searle, R.H., Nienaber, A.M.I. and Sitkin, S.B. eds., *The Routledge companion to trust*. Routledge.

Bond, R. and Smith, P.B., 1996. Culture and conformity: A meta-analysis of studies using Asch's (1952b, 1956) line judgment task. *Psychological Bulletin*, 119(1), p. 111.

Bowes-Sperry, L. and O'Leary-Kelly, A.M., 2005. To act or not to act: The dilemma faced by sexual harassment observers. *Academy of Management Review*, 30(2), pp. 288–306.

Bradley, B.H., Postlethwaite, B.E., Klotz, A.C., Hamdani, M.R. and Brown, K.G., 2012. Reaping the benefits of task conflict in teams: The critical role of team psychological safety climate. *Journal of Applied Psychology*, 97(1), p. 151.

Bresman, H. and Edmondson, A.C., 2022. Exploring the relationship between team diversity, psychological safety and team performance: Evidence from pharmaceutical drug development. Harvard Business Review [online], Available at: https://hbr.org/2022/03/exploring-the

-relationship-between-team-diversity-psychological-safety-and-team-performance [Accessed 10 July 2025].

Carmeli, A., Brueller, D. and Dutton, J.E., 2009. Learning behaviours in the workplace: The role of high-quality interpersonal relationships and psychological safety. *Systems Research and Behavioral Science: The Official Journal of the International Federation for Systems Research*, 26(1), pp. 81–98.

Castaldelli-Maia, J.M., Gallinaro, J.G. de M.E., Falcão, R.S., et al., 2019. Mental health symptoms and disorders in elite athletes: A systematic review on cultural influencers and barriers to athletes seeking treatment. British Journal of Sports Medicine, 53, pp. 707–721.

Catmull, E. and Wallace, A., 2014. *Creativity, Inc.: Overcoming the unseen forces at stand in the way of true inspiration*. Bantam.

Cauwelier, P., Vincent, M.R. and Bennet, A., 2019. The influence of team psychological safety on team knowledge creation: A study with french and American engineering teams. *Journal of Knowledge Management*, 23(6), pp. 1157–1175. https://doi.org/10.1108/JKM-07-2018-0420

Chandrasekaran, A. and Mishra, A., 2012. Task design, team context, and psychological safety: An empirical analysis of R&D projects in high technology organizations. *Production and Operations Management*, 21(6), pp. 977–996.

Chapman, M., 2020. *Jacinda Ardern: A new kind of leader*. Black Inc.

Chenoweth, N. and Tadros, E., 2023. The inside story of PwC's tax scandal. *Australian Financial Review*, 243(7) pp. 6–7.

Chilcot, J., 2016. The Report of the Iraq Inquiry: Executive Summary. London: The Stationery Office. https://webarchive.nationalarchives.gov.uk/ukgwa/20171123123237/http://www.iraqinquiry.org.uk/media/246416/the-report-of-the-iraq-inquiry_executive-summary.pdf

Clegg, C.W., Robinson, M.A., Davis, M.C., Bolton, L.E., Pieniazek, R.L. and McKay, A., 2017. Applying organizational psychology as a design science: A method for predicting malfunctions in socio-technical systems (PreMiSTS). *Design Science*, 3, p. e6.

Constantin, R.M. and Florin, S.D., 2023. An explorative study regarding the relationship between the Light Triad of personality, counterproductive work behavior and organizational citizenship behaviour. *Review of Socio-Economic Perspectives*, 8(2), pp. 19–28.

Darley, J.M. and Latané, B., 1968. Bystander intervention in emergencies: Diffusion of responsibility. *Journal of Personality and Social Psychology*, 8(41), p. 377.

Duhigg, C., 2016. What Google learned from its quest to build the perfect team. *The New York Times Magazine*, 26, p. 2016.

Edmondson, A.C., 1999. Psychological safety and learning behavior in work teams. *Administrative Science Quarterly*, 44(2), pp. 350–383.

Edmondson, A.C., 2002. *Managing the risk of learning: Psychological safety in work teams* (pp. 255–275). Cambridge, MA: Division of Research, Harvard Business School.

Edmondson, A.C., 2012. *Teaming: How organizations learn, innovate, and compete in the knowledge economy.* John Wiley & Sons.

Edmondson, A.C., 2018. *The fearless organization: Creating psychological safety in the workplace for learning, innovation, and growth.* Wiley.

Edmondson, A.C. and Besieux, T., 2021. Reflections: voice and silence in workplace conversations. *Journal of Change Management*, 21(3), pp. 269–286.

Edmondson, A.C., Kramer, R.M. and Cook, K.S., 2004. Psychological safety, trust, and learning in organizations: A group-level lens. *Trust and Distrust in Organizations: Dilemmas and Approaches*, 12, pp. 239–272.

Erkutlu, H. and Chafra, J., 2015. The mediating roles of psychological safety and employee voice on the relationship between conflict management styles and organizational identification. *American Journal of Business*, 30(1), pp. 72–91.

Fischer, P., Krueger, J.I., Greitemeyer, T., Vogrincic, C., Kastenmüller, A., Frey, D., Heene, M., Wicher, M. and Kainbacher, M., 2011. The bystander-effect: A meta-analytic review on bystander intervention in dangerous and non-dangerous emergencies. *Psychological Bulletin*, 137(4), p. 517.

Fransen, K., McEwan, D. and Sarkar, M., 2020. The impact of identity leadership on team functioning and well-being in team sport: Is psychological safety the missing link?. *Psychology of Sport and Exercise*, 51, p. 101763.

Franzen, A. and Mader, S., 2023. The power of social influence: A replication and extension of the Asch experiment. *PLoS One*, 18(11), p. e0294325.

Frazier, M.L., Fainshmidt, S., Klinger, R.L., Pezeshkan, A. and Vracheva, V., 2017. Psychological safety: A meta-analytic review and extension. *Personnel Psychology*, 70(1), pp. 113–165

Freeman, R.B. and Medoff, J.L., 1979. The two faces of unionism. *Public Interest*, 57, pp. 69–93.

From nerves to neuroses. 2019, June 12. https://www.sciencemuseum.org.uk/objects-and-stories/medicine/nerves-neuroses#:~:text=Museum%20Group%20Collection-,The%20nervous%20breakdown,George%20III%20assured%20his%20court.

Gallo, A., 2023. What is psychological safety? Harvard Business Review, July–August, pp. 70–77. Available at: https://hbr.org/2023/07/what-is-psychological-safety [Accessed 10 July 2025].

Gansberg, M., 1964. 37 who saw murder didn't call the police. *New York Times*, p. 27.

Giphart, R. and Van Vugt, M., 2018. *Mismatch: How our stone age brain deceives us every day (and what we can do about it).* Robinson

Gorden, W.I., 1988. Range of employee voice. *Employee Responsibilities and Rights Journal*, 1, pp. 283–299.

Haslam, S.A., Reicher, S.D. and Van Bavel, J.J., 2019. Rethinking the nature of cruelty: The role of identity leadership in the Stanford prison experiment. *American Psychologist*, 74(7), p. 809.

Hebles, M., Trincado-Munoz, F. and Ortega, K., 2022. Stress and turnover intentions within healthcare teams: The mediating role of psychological safety, and the moderating effect of COVID-19 worry and supervisor support. *Frontiers in Psychology*, 12, p. 758438.

Hirschman, A.O., 1970. *Exit, voice, and loyalty: Responses to decline in firms, organizations, and states.* Harvard University Press.

Hosseini, E. and Sabokro, M., 2022. A systematic literature review of the organizational voice. *Interdisciplinary Journal of Management Studies (Formerly known as Iranian Journal of Management Studies)*, 15(2), pp. 227–252.

House of Commons Liaison Committee Oral evidence: Follow-up to the Chilcott report, HC689 2 November 2016.

Ibarra, H., 1992. Homophily and differential returns: Sex differences in network structure and access in an advertising firm. *Administrative Science Quarterly*, 37(3), pp. 422–447.

Janis, I.L., 1982. *Groupthink*. 2nd ed. Boston: Houghton Mifflin.

Kahn, W.A., 1990. Psychological conditions of personal engagement and disengagement at work. *Academy of Management Journal*, 33(4), pp. 692–724.

Kandola, B., 2018. *Racism at work: The danger of indifference* (p. 101). Oxford: Pearn Kandola Publishing.

Kaufman, S.B., Yaden, D.B., Hyde, E. and Tsukayama, E., 2019. The light vs. dark triad of personality: Contrasting two very different profiles of human nature. *Frontiers in Psychology*, 10, p. 467.

Latané, B. and Darley, J.M., 1969. Bystander "apathy". *American Scientist*, 57(2), pp. 244–268.

Latané, B. and Darley, J.M., 1970. Social determinants of bystander intervention in emergencies. In: J. Macauley and L. Berkowitz, eds. Altruism and Helping Behavior. New York: Academic Press, pp. 13–27.

Latané, B. and Nida, S., 1981. Ten years of research on group size and helping. *Psychological Bulletin*, 89(2), p. 308.

Lazarsfeld, P.F.and Merton, R.K., 1954. Friendship as a social process: a substantive and methodological analysis. In Berger, M. ed., *Freedom and control in modern society* (pp. 18–66). New York: Van Nostrand.

Le Texier, T., 2019. Debunking the Stanford prison experiment. *American Psychologist*, 74(7), p. 823.

LeBreton, J.M., Shiverdecker, L.K. and Grimaldi, E.M., 2018. The dark triad and workplace behavior. *Annual Review of Organizational Psychology and Organizational Behavior*, 5(1), pp. 387–414.

Lechner, A. and Tobias Mortlock, J.M., 2022. How to create psychological safety in virtual teams. Organizational Dynamics, 51(2), Article 100880. https://doi.org/10.1016/j.orgdyn.2021.100880

Lee, H., 2021. Changes in workplace practices during the COVID-19 pandemic: The roles of emotion, psychological safety and organisation support. *Journal of Organizational Effectiveness: People and Performance*, 8(1), pp. 97–128.

LePine, J.A. and Van Dyne, L., 1998. Predicting voice behavior in work groups. *Journal of Applied Psychology*, 83(6), p. 853.

Leroy, H., Dierynck, B., Anseel, F., Simons, T., Halbesleben, J.R., McCaughey, D., Savage, G.T. and Sels, L., 2012. Behavioral integrity for safety, priority of safety, psychological safety, and patient safety: A team-level study. *Journal of Applied Psychology*, 97(6), p. 1273.

Levine, M., Taylor, P.J. and Best, R., 2011. Third parties, violence, and conflict resolution: The role of group size and collective action in the microregulation of violence. *Psychological Science*, 22(3), pp. 406–412.

Liang, J.G. and Peters-Hawkins, A.L., 2017. "I am more than what I look alike" Asian American women in public school administration. *Educational Administration Quarterly*, 53(1), pp. 40–69.

Liang, J.G., Farh, C.I. and Farh, J.L., 2012. Psychological antecedents of promotive and prohibitive voice: A two-wave examination. *Academy of Management Journal*, 55(1), pp. 71–92.

Lind, E. A., 2018. Trust and fairness. In Searle, R.H., Nienaber, A.M.I. and Sitkin, S.B. eds., *The Routledge companion to trust*. Routledge.

Lukianoff, G. and Haidt, J., 2018. *The coddling of the American mind: How good intentions and bad ideas are setting up a generation for failure*. Allen Lane.

Manning, R., Levine, M. and Collins, A., 2007. The Kitty Genovese murder and the social psychology of helping: The parable of the 38 witnesses. *American Psychologist*, 62(6), p. 555.

McAllister, D.J., 1995. Affect-and cognition-based trust as foundations for interpersonal cooperation in organizations. *Academy of Management Journal*, 38(1), pp. 24–59.

Mehra, A. Kilduff, M. and Brass, D.J., 1998. At the margins: A distinctiveness approach to the social identity and social networks of underrepresented groups. *Academy of Management Journal*, 41(4), pp. 441–452.

Milgram, S., 1974. *Obedience to authority: An experimental view*. New York: Harper and Row.

Mill, J.S., 1859. *On liberty*. Garden City, NY: Dover Thrift Editions.

Mori, K. and Arai, M., 2010. No need to fake it: Reproduction of the Asch experiment without confederates. *International Journal of Psychology*, 45(5), pp. 390–397.

Nadella S., 2017. *Hit refresh: The quest to rediscover Microsoft's soul and imagine a better future for everyone.* New York, NY: Harper Collins.

Newman, A., Donohue, R. and Eva, N., 2017. Psychological safety: A systematic review of the literature. *Human Resource Management Review*, 27(3), pp. 521–535.

Noort, M.C., Reader, T.W. and Gillespie, A. 2021. Safety voice and safety listening during aviation accidents: Cockpit voice recordings reveal that speaking-up to power is not enough. *Safety Science*, 139, pp. 105260-.

Ntoumanis, N., Dølven, S., Barkoukis, V., Boardley, I.D., Hvidemose, J.S., Juhl, C.B. and Gucciardi, D.F., 2024. Psychosocial predictors of doping intentions and use in sport and exercise: A systematic review and meta-analysis. *British Journal of Sports Medicine*, 58(19), pp. 1145–1156.

O'donovan, R. and Mcauliffe, E., 2020. A systematic review of factors that enable psychological safety in healthcare teams. *International Journal for Quality in Health Care*, 32(4), pp. 240–250.

Opoku, M.A., Choi, S.B. and Kang, S.W., 2020. Psychological safety in Ghana: Empirical analyses of antecedents and consequences. *International Journal of Environmental Research and Public Health*, 17(1), p. 214.

Pasmore, W. Foreword to Edgar Schein: Learning Through Helping in Coghlan, D., 2024. *Edgar H. Schein: The artistry of a reflexive organizational scholar-practitioner.* Taylor & Francis.

Paulhus, D.L. and Williams, K.M., 2002. The dark triad of personality: Narcissism, Machiavellianism, and psychopathy. *Journal of Research in Personality*, 36(6), pp. 556–563.

Perkins, K., Ghosh, S., Vera, J., Aragon, C. and Hyland, A., 2022. The persistence of safety silence: How flight deck microcultures influence the efficacy of crew resource management. *International Journal of Aviation, Aeronautics, and Aerospace*, 9(3), p. 6.

Rao, H., Sutton, R. and Webb, A.P., 2008. Innovation lessons from Pixar: An interview with Oscar-winning director Brad Bird. *McKinsey Quarterly*, 4(1), pp. 1–9.

Rauthmann, J.F., 2012. Towards multifaceted Machiavellianism: Content, factorial, and construct validity of a German Machiavellianism Scale. *Personality and Individual Differences*, 52(3), pp. 345–351.

Robison. P., 2021. *Flying blind: The 737 MAX tragedy, and the fall of boeing.* Penguin Business

Rousseau, D.M., Sitkin, S.B., Burt, R.S. and Camerer, C., 1998. Not so different after all: A cross-discipline view of trust. *Academy of Management Review*, 23(3), pp. 393–404.

Schein, E.H. and Bennis, W.G., 1965. *Personal and organizational change through group methods: The laboratory approach.* Wiley.

Schein, E.H. and Schein, P., 2017. *Organisational culture and leadership*. 5th ed. Hoboken, NJ: John Wiley & Sons.

Seal, M., 2021. Leave the gun, take the cannoli: The epic story of the making of the godfather.

Searle, R.H. and Rice, C., 2025. Trust, and high control: an exploratory study of Counterproductive Work Behaviour in a high security organization. *European Journal of Work and Organizational Psychology*, 34(3), pp. 392–402.

Senge, P.M., 1990. *The fifth discipline: The art and practice of the learning organization*. London: Random House.

Shanmugaratnam, A., McLaren, C.D., Schertzinger, M. and Bruner, M.W., 2024. Exploring the relationship between coach-initiated motivational climate and athlete well-being, resilience, and psychological safety in competitive sport teams. *International Journal of Sports Science & Coaching*, p. 17479541241278602.

Sjöblom, K., Mäkiniemi, J.P. and Mäkikangas, A., 2022. "I was given three marks and told to buy a porsche"—supervisors' experiences of leading psychosocial safety climate and team psychological safety in a remote academic setting. *International Journal of Environmental Research and Public Health*, 19(19), p. 12016.

Smith, S.F. and Lilienfeld, S.O., 2013. Psychopathy in the workplace: The knowns and unknowns. *Aggression and Violent Behavior*, 18(2), pp. 204–218.

Sue, D.W., 2009. *Microaggressions in everyday life: Race, gender and sexual orientation*. New York: John Wiley.

Tajfel, H. and Turner, J.C., 1979. An integrative theory of inter-group conflict. In Austin, W. and Worschel, S. eds., *The social psychology of intergroup relations*. Monterey, CA: Brooks/Cole Publishing Company.

Takano, Y. and Sogon, S., 2008. Are Japanese more collectivistic than Americans? Examining conformity in in-groups and the reference-group effect. *Journal of Cross-Cultural Psychology*, 39, pp. 237–250.

Taylor, J., 2020. *How discrimination affects our performance in free to soar: Race and well-being in organisations*. Oxford: Pearn Kandola Publishing.

Tkalich, A., Šmite, D., Andersen, N.H. and Moe, N.B., 2022. What happens to psychological safety when going remote?. *IEEE Software*, 41(1), pp. 113–122.

Twenge, Jean M., 2017. *IGen: Why today's super-connected kids are growing up less rebellious, more tolerant, less happy-- and completely unprepared for adulthood (and what this means for the rest of Us)*. Atria Books.

Usto, M., Drace, S. and Hadziahmetovic, N., 2019. Replication of the «Asch Effect» in Bosnia and Herzegovina: Evidence for the moderating role of group similarity in conformity. *Psihologijske Teme*, 28, pp. 589–599.

Vakira, E., Shereni, N.C., Ncube, C.M. and Ndlovu, N., 2023. The effect of inclusive leadership on employee engagement, mediated by psychological safety in the hospitality industry. African Journal of Hospitality, Tourism and Leisure, 12(2), pp. 484–500.

Vella, S.A., Mayland, E., Schweickle, M.J., Sutcliffe, J.T., McEwan, D. and Swann, C., 2024. Psychological safety in sport: A systematic review and concept analysis. *International Review of Sport and Exercise Psychology*, 17(1), pp. 516–539.

Walsh, D., 2007. *From lance to landis: Inside the American doping controversy at the Tour de France*. Ballantine Books.

Walsh, D., 2013. *Seven deadly sins: My pursuit of lance Armstrong*. Simon & Schuster.

Weiner, J., Francois, C., Stone-Johnson, C. and Childs, J., 2021. Keep safe, keep learning: principals' role in creating psychological safety and organizational learning during the COVID-19 pandemic. In: Frontiers in Education, 5, Article 618483. Lausanne: Frontiers Media SA. https://doi .org/10.3389/feduc.2020.618483

Wietrak, E. and Gifford, J., 2024. *Trust and psychological safety: An evidence review*. Chartered Institute of Personnel and Development.

Wilhelm, H., Richter, A.W. and Semrau, T., 2019. Employee learning from failure: A team-as-resource perspective. *Organization Science (Providence, R.I.)*, 30(4), pp. 694–714.

Williams, J.D., Woodson, A.N. and Wallace, T.L., 2016. "Can we say the n-word?": Exploring psychological safety during race talk. *Research in Human Development*, 13(1), pp. 15–31.

Williams, M., 2022. *The science of hate: How prejudice becomes hate and what we can do to stop it*. London: London Faber and Faber.

Wright, B., 1963. *Physical disability: A psychological approach* (p. 118). New York: Harper & Row.

Wu, P.P.Y., Babaei, T., O'Shea, M., Mengersen, K., Drovandi, C., McGibbon, K.E., Pyne, D.B., Mitchell, L.J. and Osborne, M.A., 2021. Predicting performance in 4 x 200-m freestyle swimming relay events. *PLoS One*, 16(7), p. e0254538.

Zimbardo, P., 2008. *The lucifer effect*. New York, NY: Random House.

For Product Safety Concerns and Information please contact our EU
representative GPSR@taylorandfrancis.com
Taylor & Francis Verlag GmbH, Kaufingerstraße 24, 80331 München, Germany

BUILDING A PSYCHOLOGICALLY SAFE WORK ENVIRONMENT

Building a Psychologically Safe Work Environment provides a roadmap to enable the creation of spaces in organizations where voices are heard, actions taken, and lives improved. Written in an approachable question-and-answer format, the book offers a valuable "dip in and out" approach to questions surrounding psychological safety in professional life.

Written by an expert business psychologist, it provides guidance on such topics as what psychological safety is, why it is important, how to tell if you work in a psychologically safe environment, and what actions leaders can take to make their workplace more psychologically safe. Through an examination of current research and in-depth analysis of real-life examples, the book takes a systemic approach that equips you with the tools to make the changes in your own workplace that will have the greatest impact on your teams and yourself. In so doing, it empowers you to create an inclusive work environment that is engaging, respectful, challenging, and effective.

Making the concept of psychological safety easily accessible and offering tips on how to increase psychological safety within your own workplace, this is the ideal guide for leaders of all levels, from those first stepping up to seasoned managers.

Binna Kandola is co-founder and Senior Partner at Pearn Kandola, a practice of Business Psychologists. He is Visiting Professor at Leeds University Business School, UK, and has spent over 40 years researching diversity, inclusion, and bias in the workplace. As a practitioner, he has worked with some of the world's leading organizations, including American Express, Microsoft, NATO, and the World Bank. He has been on the UK's Asian Power List for the last six years.

BPS ASK THE EXPERTS IN PSYCHOLOGY SERIES

British Psychological Society

Routledge, in partnership with the British Psychological Society (BPS), is pleased to present BPS Ask the Experts, a new popular science series that addresses key issues and answers the burning questions. Drawing on the expertise of established psychologists, every book in the series provides authoritative and straightforward guidance on pressing topics that matter to real people in their everyday lives.

All books in the BPS Ask the Experts series are written for the reader with no prior knowledge or experience. For answers to everything you ever wanted to know about issues important to you, ask the expert!

For more information about this series, please visit: BPS Ask The Experts in Psychology Series - Book Series - Routledge & CRC Press

BUILDING A PSYCHOLOGICALLY SAFE WORK ENVIRONMENT

BINNA KANDOLA

Routledge
Taylor & Francis Group

LONDON AND NEW YORK

Designed cover image: Getty Images

First published 2026
by Routledge
4 Park Square, Milton Park, Abingdon, Oxon OX14 4RN

and by Routledge
605 Third Avenue, New York, NY 10158

Routledge is an imprint of the Taylor & Francis Group, an informa business

© 2026 Binna Kandola

The right of Binna Kandola to be identified as author of this work has been asserted in accordance with sections 77 and 78 of the Copyright, Designs and Patents Act 1988.

British Library Cataloguing-in-Publication Data
A catalogue record for this book is available from the British Library

ISBN: 9781032818825 (hbk)
ISBN: 9781032818818 (pbk)
ISBN: 9781003501855 (ebk)

DOI: 10.4324/9781003501855

Typeset in Bembo
by Deanta Global Publishing Services, Chennai, India

To Jo Kandola—my (psychologically) safe haven.

CONTENTS

PART III   THE SYSTEMIC VIEW